T0100383

SWAB

SWAB

LEADERSHIP IN THE RACE
TO PROVIDE COVID TESTING TO AMERICA

JON R. COHEN, MD

Skyhorse Publishing

Skyhorse Publishing books may be purchased in bulk at special discounts for sales promotion, corporate gifts, fund-raising, or educational purposes. Special editions can also be created to specifications. For details, contact the Special Sales Department, Skyhorse Publishing, 307 West 36th Street, 11th Floor, New York, NY 10018 or info@skyhorsepublishing.com.

Skyhorse® and Skyhorse Publishing® are registered trademarks of Skyhorse Publishing, Inc.®, a Delaware corporation.

Visit our website at www.skyhorsepublishing.com.

10 9 8 7 6 5 4 3 2 1

Library of Congress Cataloging-in-Publication Data is available on file.

Cover design by David Ter-Avanesyan
Jacket photograph by Shutterstock

ISBN: 978-1-5107-7843-6
Ebook ISBN: 978-1-5107-7846-7

Printed in the United States of America

For my wife of forty-two years, Karen, my daughter, Leslie, my son-in-law, Brendan, my grandson, Jackson, and my granddaughter, Colette, for making life so incredibly wonderful.

"COVID is where intuition goes to die."

—attribution unknown

"You can accomplish anything in life, provided that you do not mind who gets the credit."

—Harry Truman

Contents

Glossary   xi

Introduction   xiii

Chapter 1: Sorry, but You're on Your Own   1
Leadership Reflection #1: Listen to the Little Man.   9

Chapter 2: The First Week: A Crash Course in Drive-Through Testing   11
Leadership Reflection #2: Be Nice, Be Helpful, and Stay in Touch.   23

Chapter 3: Making Pancakes   25
Leadership Reflection #3: Keep Your Hand on the Pulse and Live with Uncertainty.   36

Chapter 4: "My Kingdom for a Swab"   39
Leadership Reflection #4: Protect Your Reputation Regardless of Costs.   52

Chapter 5: Teamwork for a Slam Dunk in the NBA Bubble   53
Leadership Reflection #5: Pick Talented People and Stay Out of Their Way.   65

Chapter 6: 4th and Long   67
Leadership Reflection #6: Respond to a Crisis with Honesty.   89

Chapter 7: School Testing: Reading, Writing, Swabbing, and Arithmetic   **91**

    Leadership Reflection #7: Frequently Wrong, but Never
in Doubt.   102

Chapter 8: "The Love Boat"   **103**

    Leadership Reflection #8: Walk the Walk Before You Talk
the Talk.   115

Chapter 9: I Need a Test, and I Want It *Now*   **117**

    Leadership Reflection #9: The Enemy of Courage Is Fear.   131

Chapter 10: Moving Forward: Fixes for the Future   **133**

    Leadership Reflection #10: Communicate Often.   141

Acknowledgments   *143*

About the Author   *145*

Index   *147*

Glossary

Analyzers/platforms/machines: These terms are used interchangeably to describe the machines that run the COVID-19 test in a laboratory.

Antigen-based devices: Devices that look for easily detectable proteins that attach to the surface of the virus but are less accurate then PCR tests. These tests are extremely reliable if a person tests positive. However, these tests are relatively unreliable if the patient tests negative. In other words, if a patient has symptoms and tests negative with an antigen test, it is unreliable as an indicator of not having COVID-19.

COVID-19: The disease people get when infected with SARS-CoV-2 virus.

Home tests: Tests that can be run at home or anywhere on-site. They are simple to use and give a quick result. Most have been antigen-based but some use PCR technology. The individual swabs their nose, usually places the swab in a receptacle, adds a chemical developer, and waits to see if the indicator is positive.

PCR (polymerase chain reaction): The process used to detect the presence of the virus. PCR works by repeatedly doubling any existing viral RNA present in a specimen until it has been magnified to a level where the virus becomes detectable. PCR is a highly accurate process, is usually performed in a laboratory, and is the "gold standard" for testing viral presence. If a patient tests negative with a PCR test it is very reliable in determining that the patient does not have COVID-19 and vice versa, if the patient tests positive, regardless of whether the patient does or does not have symptoms, that patient has COVID-19.

Point-of-care devices (POC): Devices that are used on location to test for the virus. Point-of-care devices can use PCR technology or antigen technology. PCR-based POC devices are more accurate then antigen-based devices. Some POC devices can be run by the patient with little instruction whereas some POC devices may require specific training.

Rapid testing: Frequently used as synonymous with POC testing as the result is usually available within thirty minutes.

SARS-CoV-2: The virus that causes the disease called COVID-19.

Introduction

I was one year into my tenure as CEO and executive chairman of BioReference Laboratories, one of the largest diagnostic laboratories in the country, when the new coronavirus (Sars-CoV-2) causing the disease that became known as COVID-19 morphed into a full-fledged worldwide pandemic. By the beginning of March 2020, it became clear to me that the federal government had made no preparations for the country to test millions and millions of people during a pandemic and certainly had no plan to engage commercial laboratories like BioReference to assist in that effort.

SWAB goes behind the scenes to tell the story of how BioReference Laboratories—working with no road map, no federal guidance or support, and no prior pandemic experience—established processes to provide testing to every imaginable segment of the American public including cities, counties, states, hospitals, physicians, nursing homes, federally qualified health centers (FQHCs), urgent care facilities, public schools, colleges, employers and manufacturers of all types, entertainment companies and public venues, professional sports teams, movie production companies, cruise ships, casinos, prisons, airlines, and, of course, the general public. BioReference outmaneuvered competition ten times its size and rose to national prominence as the "first" on many COVID-19 testing frontiers: the first and the exclusive provider that allowed the NBA to complete their season in the "Bubble"; the first and exclusive provider of the testing that allowed the NFL to play 256 games, the playoffs, and the Super Bowl; the first to perform testing for New York City Public Schools, the largest school system in the country, allowing hundreds of thousands of students to return to their classrooms; provide testing for the first cruise ship to sail (Royal Caribbean) when the CDC order was lifted allowing cruise lines to sail again, and eventually where we tested as many as twenty-four ships out of eight ports every day; the first and the exclusive provider of the testing that allowed the National Hockey League, Major League Soccer, and a majority of the Major League Baseball teams to keep playing through their seasons; the first to test thousands of fans so they could attend a playoff game (Buffalo Bills versus the Indianapolis Colts), and the first to develop large-scale testing programs for testing thousands of people within one hour of special events they were attending at Madison Square Garden in Manhattan, the Chase Center in San Francisco, and Barclays Center in Brooklyn, New York.

SWAB is the first book to tell the story of COVID-19 testing and is an important component in the historic record of a once-in-a-century pandemic. BioReference grew from four thousand to eight thousand employees over four months. Two years later, the company had performed over twenty-five million lab-based COVID-19 tests and was recognized as the nation's leader in surveillance testing (rapid point-of-care testing). The story describes the many people, the hundreds of operational issues, the details of how we eventually developed the capacity to perform 100,000 COVID-19 tests a day, and how the company addressed an unpredictable series of seemingly insurmountable obstacles.

SWAB is also a business "case study" of management and leadership during a different type of crisis. Most crisis events are singular in nature whereby the management team must make decisions based on the ramifications of a defined event. COVID-19 was different as the crisis continued to evolve; events on the ground changed daily as the virus spread from city to city, technology to test the virus evolved at an unprecedented rate, opinions as to who should or should not get tested changed and varied from industry to industry, and public reaction to getting tested for the virus changed. All of this occurred while multiple variables that impacted on our ability to consistently deliver the test results were out of our control. In each chapter I relate the story of how the executive team with me managed the crisis where the only certainty seemed to be that everyday something changed from the prior day. The quote at the beginning of the book, "COVID is where intuition goes to die!" stayed on the whiteboard in my office for two years as every time we thought we knew what was going to happen next, we were invariably wrong. As stories of the company's innovative testing solutions unfold, I reflect at the end of each chapter on how the events in that chapter are related to a specific leadership strategy.

Healthcare workers and professionals, as well as all the Americans who spent time searching online for access to a test or waiting somewhere in a testing line, deserve to hear the full story of COVID-19 testing during the pandemic and to understand that solutions exist to prevent this nation from ever suffering a testing debacle like the one we saw with COVID-19. I tell this story now with the hope that we can all learn from both the successes and the mistakes those of us at BioReference made during our long fight against COVID-19, and thereby be better prepared to handle the next pandemic when and if we have one. In the last chapter I make some recommendations on how I believe we should prepare for the next pandemic.

Finally, I tell this story because of the extraordinary strength, courage, creativity, and stamina of the members of the various BioReference teams that organized almost overnight to take on the challenges at hand. These people worked 24/7 performing many strange and new tasks under the most stressful conditions for almost two straight years, barely ever resting. They deserve to be acknowledged and thanked for their hard work.

CHAPTER 1

Sorry, but You're on Your Own

Every generation has its milestone moments, those bigger-than-life events that people all around the world experience together and then later use as reference points in their individual and collective lives. Where were you when Neil Armstrong walked on the moon? When President Kennedy was assassinated? When the World Trade Center went down? The recent COVID-19 pandemic created a new milestone moment for people everywhere: Where were you the first time you sat in your car or stood in a long line, wearing a mask, waiting to get "swabbed"—an incredibly unpleasant experience during which someone sticks an elongated Q-tip way up your nose toward your brain?

For many people, their encounter with the little cotton-tipped stick placed up into their nose collecting a nasal specimen for a COVID-19 test launched an avalanche of anxieties: Do I have COVID-19 or not? When will I get my result, and what will I do if I am positive? If I am positive, could I have infected other people? Am I going to wind up in the hospital? For many, the first time they were swabbed for COVID-19 was also the first time they realized that they could die from a disease they had never even heard of a few weeks earlier. The brief but uncomfortable nasal "swab" awakened a realization of their own mortality.

When COVID-19 hit, I was the CEO and Executive Chairman of BioReference Laboratories, a New Jersey–based OPKO-Health diagnostic company, and my "this new virus is going to be a really big effing deal" moment probably came earlier than it did for most. It was Friday, February 28, 2020, and I was getting ready to attend the rehearsal dinner for the wedding of my closest friend Paul's middle daughter Elizabeth at the Indian Creek Country Club on a private island off Miami Beach. My phone rang as I reached for my tie. It was Jim.

Jim Weisberger, MD, a brilliant anatomic and clinical pathologist, is the chief medical officer and lab director for BioReference Laboratories. He has been with the company for over twenty years, and he knows everything there is to know about clinical laboratory medicine and how laboratories function. He understands all the intricate science behind the more than 3,000 different tests that our labs routinely run and every detail about how the various machines (also known as "platforms" or "analyzers") that run the tests work. I had only been CEO at BioReference for a year, but I had already learned that Jim is both practical and creative, and that he has a wonderfully dark and sarcastic sense of humor. If you ask Jim to do something, his answer invariably will be: "That's impossible, that's an idiotic idea, total bullshit, that's never going to work, there's no way that it makes any sense." But then several days later, Jim will come back and say, "You know that thing that we talked about? Well, I figured it out and I think I can make it work." I knew that Jim could get anything done if I just left him alone. I also knew that, as a rule, Jim only called me when something pretty bad was amiss.

About a month earlier, in late January, Jim and I and other members of the executive team at BioReference had gathered for our first serious discussion about whether or not we should develop a test for the novel coronavirus pathogen, called COVID-19. The virus had been spreading in Asia and Europe, and on January 20, the first US case of the disease had been confirmed in Seattle, Washington. At our executive meeting, some people believed that the new virus would be "just like Zika. A flash in the pan." At the time there were many people, some of them quite prominent, who agreed. Although COVID-19 had already infected 81,000 people globally and killed almost 3,000, concerns about potential health risks in the United States remained low. Only two days before Jim called me in Miami, President Trump had announced at a White House press conference that Vice President Mike Pence would coordinate the government's response to the coronavirus. During his announcement, the president had insisted that "the risk to the American people remains very low. . . . We're testing everybody that we need to test, and we're finding very little problem, very little problem." The new virus was increasingly a topic in the news, but at that point the focus was not so much on possible health risks for Americans, but on the economic harm it might cause. A *New York Times* front-page piece that ran on February 27 warned readers that "Coronavirus Fears Drive Stocks Down for 6th Day."[1]

Despite the Trump administration's seeming lack of alarm about the virus, and some hesitation from a few members of the executive team, I decided that we should move forward and start researching and developing a plan to test for the virus. If the need for testing became real, I didn't want to lose several weeks in development and the cost to us was minimal. Under the official US protocol for outbreak of any new disease, the Centers for Disease Control and Prevention (CDC) are tasked with developing a test for the new virus and then produce and send their test kits to the public health labs around the country. This delegation of testing development and distribution by the CDC to public health labs had worked well enough during other outbreaks, including Ebola, Zika, H1N1, and SARS, also known as bird flu. But recently, given the speed with which the new virus was spreading, the CDC had decided that in the case of the coronavirus it would extend testing approvals to private and commercial labs.

As the threat continued to emerge and grow every day, Jim and his lab technicians had been working around the clock in our New Jersey labs, experimenting and validating various COVID-19 testing procedures and platforms in anticipation of receiving CDC approval to begin testing for the virus. Our operations experts were redesigning our labs, which had been set up to test blood and urine samples, to allow clinical PCR testing on nasal swab samples. Our technology division was creating new programs that could identify and accession patients at drive-throughs and other sites outside the home turf of our labs, our human resources division was interviewing and hiring new people in an effort

---

1   Matt Phillips, "Coronavirus Fears Drive Stocks Down for 6th Day and into Correction," *New York Times*, February 27, 2020 (corrected February 28, 2020). nytimes.com/2020/02/27/business/stock-market-coronavirus.html.

to double our employee count, and our legal department was drowning in the paperwork for all the new contracts that city, county, state, and federal agencies required for COVID-19 testing.

As it turned out, Jim was calling me on that Friday in February to let me know that he had just received the CDC guidelines for the environmental requirements needed to run their COVID-19 test, and essentially the CDC protocols as specified would prevent almost all labs—whether public, private, or commercial—from running any COVID-19 tests. The CDC guidance stated that any laboratory performing COVID-19 tests would need to do so under Biological Safety Level Three (BSL-3) regulations, which required significant isolation techniques and specific airflow conditions and special types of hoods. These hoods are laboratory benches where a technician can work with the viral specimen in a ventilated space from behind a glass barrier that keeps any material from escaping the workspace back into the lab. BSL-3 conditions were usually reserved for highly contagious, possibly lethal infectious viruses or bacteria. The term BSL-3 conjured up images for me of scientists in science fiction movies fully outfitted in spacesuits who die instantly when there is a break in their suit. I was reminded of one of my favorite movies, *The Andromeda Strain*—released in 1971 and based on the book by Michael Crichton—in which scientists who are trying to identify and prevent the spread of a deadly extraterrestrial virus work in a BSL-3 environment under laboratory hoods similar to those the CDC was requiring for COVID-19 testing. The big problem here, and the reason Jim had called me, was that BSL-3–compliant equipment and working conditions are not possible in most labs, which typically operate under less stringent BSL-2 conditions.

That phone call from Jim was when I first realized that COVID-19 could morph into a very intense large-scale health crisis. It was also when I first suspected there might be a serious disconnect between the federal government's so-called plans for COVID-19 testing and what actually needed to be happening on the ground in real time. If the CDC was requiring stringent BSL-3 testing protocols, they must believe that the new virus was a highly contagious, potentially deadly threat to the American public. And yet they had just issued regulations that would take almost every lab in the country out of the testing game!

I hung up with Jim and called a good friend, Paul Mango, the Deputy Chief of Staff for Policy for the Department of Health and Human Services. Paul is a whip-smart healthcare leader, and the former head of McKinsey's healthcare practice. Later in the pandemic he would play a central role in the distribution of the COVID-19 vaccines through the program called Operation Warp Speed. I explained to Paul that the CDC's stringent guidelines requiring a BSL-3 lab environment would prevent almost all of the country's laboratories—whether public, private, or commercial—from performing COVID-19 testing. Within fifteen minutes of my phone call, Paul arranged a conference call with members of the CDC, the Food and Drug Administration (FDA), and members of the White House Coronavirus Task Force to share the concerns Jim and I had about the CDC's requirements. Fortunately, everyone agreed with Jim's initial assessment of the situation, and within twenty-four hours the CDC regulations had been revised: as long as you were testing in a BSL-2 lab and used certain Personal Protection Equipment (PPE) at the levels required by BSL-3 regulations, you were good to go for COVID-19 testing. Fortunately, the first major roadblock to bringing COVID-19 testing capabilities to commercial labs had been removed relatively easily. Unfortunately, in the months to come anyone trying to provide COVID-19 testing in the United States would encounter a series of frustrating roadblocks caused by the confusion and lack of guidance at the federal level.

Four days later, on March 3, I traveled to Washington, D.C., to attend the annual board of directors meeting of the American Clinical Laboratory Association (ACLA). The mood among the various ACLA members seemed fairly normal with some, but not really a lot of, talk about the new coronavirus in the conversations circulating around the room. During the meeting, quite unexpectedly, Steve Rusckowski, the CEO of Quest Diagnostics and chairman of the board of directors of ACLA, received a call inviting several of us to meet with Vice President Pence and members of the White House Coronavirus Task Force to discuss how the commercial lab industry might help provide testing during the pandemic. Seven of us, representing a variety of commercial diagnostic labs, went over to the West Wing of the White House to meet with Vice President Pence, director of the task force Dr. Deborah Birx, FDA commissioner Steven Hahn, CDC director Dr. Robert Redfield, HHS secretary Alex Azar, and domestic policy adviser Joe Grogan.

As I sat at the conference table in the West Wing's windowless Roosevelt Room, under the gaze of Theodore Roosevelt astride his horse as he looked down from his portrait hanging over the mantel, I could tell that the vice president had been prepped well for the meeting and was up to date on the issues. He asked insightful questions and was fully engaged in the conversation. More importantly, Dr. Deborah Birx, who was extremely well qualified to handle the challenges of a pandemic, was clearly the brains behind the operation. The task force was clearly asking if we would assist in providing testing but there was no substantial discussion in the meeting of how the commercial labs would be integrated into a national testing program and no solid commitment from the feds as to how they would help get the job done. Even worse, no one at the federal level ever did develop such a plan.

After the White House meeting, ACLA president Julie Khani released a statement about the meeting and urged the administration and Congress to expand emergency use authorizations (EUAs) to provide clear testing guidelines and priorities for those at high risk and to "provide funding for additional testing resources and support, including the cost associated with developing and performing tests as well as acquiring necessary supplies, including adequate testing supplies for specimen collection and protective gear for lab technicians who are working on the frontlines of specimen testing." Everything in the statement sounded rational enough, doable enough. Unfortunately, there was one big problem: Almost none of it ever happened. Throughout this once-in-a-century pandemic, the message the federal government seemed to send to the diagnostic industry was: we will try to help you, stay in touch, but you folks go figure it out yourselves.

Authorities at the federal level had given no real consideration to— and thus had made no preparations for—the possibility that the country might need to test millions and millions of people during a pandemic. Because of this stunning lack of preparedness, the United States had . . .

- no plan or contingency plan for how the United States would conduct mass testing on hundreds of thousands of patients a day;

- no plan for how the American public would gain access to tests (i.e., testing sites);
- no supplies in the strategic national stockpile to assist labs in the event of a pandemic;
- no plan for how to manage the supply chain and distribute the equipment and supplies that would be needed to do high-volume testing;
- no plan to coordinate the existing patchwork of laboratories around the United States to direct testing capabilities to the areas that needed it the most;
- no single agency or person tasked with developing a well-coordinated plan to address all testing needs nationwide in the case of a serious widespread outbreak;
- no plan for how to fund the testing needs; and
- no plan for how to engage the for-profit commercial laboratories like BioReference to assist the country during a pandemic.

All hell was about to break loose, and we were on our own with no road map, no guidance, and no prior pandemic experience.

On March 5, the same day I flew home from the ACLA meetings in Washington, D.C., we issued a press release announcing that BioReference would be offering COVID-19 testing soon, possibly within a week. Usually when a diagnostic lab is going to launch a new test of any kind it must first submit all the technical data about the test to the CDC and the FDA, and then go through the complicated and difficult process of getting federal approval. But with the novel coronavirus spreading across the country at warp speed, and thousands of laboratories clamoring to get approval to test for it, the normal regulatory process was abandoned. New York had recently received permission from the CDC to run its own approval process for testing in New York labs, and soon after the CDC in essence turned to the states and said: "Screw it. You guys just go ahead and do the approvals. And if everything looks good, keep going."

On March 13, BioReference received approval from the New Jersey state government to begin COVID-19 testing. We issued a press release with two announcements: First, that we were now accepting specimens for testing for coronavirus disease from healthcare providers, clinics, and health systems throughout the United States; and second, that we would be partnering with the New York State Department of Health to provide testing at the first public drive-through testing facility on the East Coast, which was to open that same day—March 13—in New Rochelle, New York, the epicenter of the New York State outbreak.

It was all happening so fast. We had no idea what exactly would be coming next or where it would all go. But really, there was no time to think about any of that. We were off and running.

* * *

As I look back now, I can see that that weekend in February when I flew to Miami for a wedding marked a kind of turning point, not just for what was going to happen to my life and to the lives of everyone who worked at BioReference, but for what was going to happen to everyone across the country—and indeed, around the world. For one thing, although I didn't realize this in the moment, it would be a long, long time before I—or anyone else on earth—would be jumping on a plane to attend a wedding! In fact, over the next few weeks, as the COVID-19 pandemic settled like a gray blanket over the nation, everyday activities across the country would grind to a halt. Offices and schools and restaurants and theaters—and all the other places where people typically gather—would sit abandoned and empty. An eerie stillness would hover over the empty streets in cities and towns, as most people stayed isolated in their homes. But the COVID-19 pandemic would have a drastically different effect on diagnostic laboratories, as well as on many other healthcare-related industries. Instead of slowing down to an eerie state of stillness, and despite the lack of federal guidance and support, the people inside the labs and offices of BioReference and other major laboratories were about to experience unprecedentedly hectic levels of activity as they worked their way through the regulatory thickets and the chaos of the pandemic to deliver the majority of all the COVID-19 testing for the country. The nation was fortunate that Steve Rusckowski and Adam Schecter, the CEOs of Quest Diagnostics and LabCorp, the two largest labs in the country, were in their positions at the time. Both are incredibly effective leaders who successfully navigated their companies to deliver millions of COVID-19 tests to the country in our time of need.

Leadership Reflection #1: Listen to the Little Man.

I like to refer to your inner voice as the little man sitting on your shoulder talking to you all day about the right thing to do. It is easy in surgery to try and ignore that voice when evaluating patients after surgery, especially if it means taking the patient back to the operating room for a potential complication. The patient isn't doing well, has signs of infection or bleeding, and you try to rationalize that the patient will get better without reoperating. Leaders must listen to their inner voice and act without all of the facts, listen to the little man, and follow their "gut" instinct. As COVID-19 began to spread and the government began to minimize the data, minimize the potential impact of the virus, and announced we had enough testing in the nation, it just didn't feel right to me. All of the reported data and the broadcasts from other countries indicated otherwise. When the CDC first indicated that the highest precautions were needed to test for the virus to prevent possible death from exposure, it signaled to me that it was not business as usual. Somehow our brains can assimilate tremendous amounts of disparate information and signal what is the right answer. Listening to that inner voice and acting on that information is what good leaders do despite what might not be obvious to others.

CHAPTER 2

The First Week: A Crash Course in Drive-Through Testing

On a Saturday evening in early March 2020, my wife Karen called me into our living room to watch a CNN story about a new drive-through site for coronavirus testing that had been launched at Kyungpook National University's Chilgok Hospital in South Korea. Patients would line up in their vehicles and wait for their turn to drive up to a tollbooth-like station where they would stop and open their car window so that a nurse (in full PPE) could swab their nose and throat. "That," said Karen, "looks like a very efficient way to get people tested for COVID-19."

After forty-two years of marriage, I know that Karen is usually correct when it comes to most things, including evaluating efficiency. Karen's junior high school friends will tell you that she is the smartest person they have ever known. She was accepted to Harvard University, but turned the offer down to attend Boston University where she could complete a combined program of college and medical school in six years. Her parents never forgave her for turning down Harvard, but she did okay. She is currently chief of breast surgery for Northwell Health System and one of the most successful breast cancer surgeons in the country. Karen is almost always correct, but neither Karen nor I had any idea how quickly her assessment of the drive-through COVID-19 testing in South Korea would be validated—with BioReference's help—right here in New York.

Four days after Karen had called me over to watch that TV story, on March 9, I received a phone call from New York's governor Andrew Cuomo. Governor Cuomo wanted to know whether BioReference could provide testing resources to support the rapidly expanding epidemic in New York State. The state, although it had several hundred health systems as well as commercial and public health labs, could only do a couple hundred tests per day; most hospitals were using whatever limited testing capacity they had for their own patients and staff. They were in no position to test the general public. BioReference had not yet received official approval to begin testing—in fact, we had announced our plan to begin COVID-19 testing as soon as possible only four days earlier. But I assured Governor Cuomo that once we received approval to test—and after making sure any ICU patients, healthcare workers, and other frontline workers who needed testing had been taken care of—I would divert as much of our daily testing capacity as possible to the state's general population. I estimated that we would probably be able to provide New York with at least 5,000 tests per day.

Governor Cuomo had another request. In addition to having our lab run tests on specimens collected from various New York health facilities, he wanted to know if BioReference would provide testing for several drive-through testing sites, first in New Rochelle, ground zero for the outbreak in New York, and then at several other locations around the state. I couldn't remember having been to a drive-through of any kind in my life, but I told Governor Cuomo yes, we would take on drive-through testing.

The four days following my call with Governor Cuomo were overwhelmingly busy in all of our offices and labs as various teams worked not only to validate the different platforms we would use for COVID-19 testing, but also to organize the logistical systems and staff we would need to provide testing for six drive-through testing lanes in a parking lot in New Rochelle, to transport all the New York specimens (from both the drive-through site and various New York healthcare facilities) to our New Jersey laboratories, to log in the specimens (called accessioning), to test the specimens, and then to report the results back to the state, the county, the city, the CDC, the patients, and the patients' physicians.

During this very busy time, Natalie Cummins, our SVP and Chief Commercial Officer, heard that Governor Cuomo had invited me to join him in New Rochelle on March 13 for the opening of the first drive-through on the East Coast. She was horrified. How could I even consider attending an event located in a COVID-19 "hot spot"? It was the earliest days of pandemic awareness, and fear about the highly infectious nature of the COVID-19 virus seemed to be spreading as quickly as the virus itself. Natalie soon realized that I was determined to be at the opening of the drive-through site, and when I inadvertently let it drop that I could not recall having been to a drive-through of any kind, her horror quickly morphed into amusement. She insisted on initiating me to the drive-through experience by taking me to a Dunkin' Donuts next to our offices in Elmwood Park, New Jersey, before I headed off to New Rochelle.

Only four days after he had contacted me about testing, on March 13, I joined Governor Cuomo and his team as we prepared to open the first drive-through COVID-19 testing site on the East Coast in the parking lot of Glen Island State Park in New Rochelle, New York. Five of us had gathered for the press conference: Governor Cuomo; Michael Dowling, the CEO of Northwell Health, the largest healthcare provider in New York State; Simonida Subotic, New York State's deputy secretary for economic development; Mike Kopy, New York State's director of emergency management; and me. We all stood in the light drizzle in a temporary tent in front of United States and New York State flags and watched as long lines of cars with people waiting to be tested stacked up in six lanes across the parking lot, as well as down the highway for as far as the eye could see.

Now, as I watched the six lanes of cars begin to move through the lot, I noted that these drive-through stations were nothing like what I had experienced at Dunkin' Donuts that week, and nothing like what the American public experiences whenever they grab a fast-food fix at some drive-through establishment. With no menu to scrutinize and no piped-in voice asking for your order, these testing stations had been designed for efficiency. They resembled highway tollbooth plazas, where multiple lanes of traffic pass through simultaneously, more than a single lane fast-food or banking drive-through. In this case, each "tollbooth" consisted of a tented area that had a table loaded with the supplies that would allow a medical attendant, dressed in full PPE, to swab someone's nose in less than ten seconds once they had pulled up in their car, rolled down the car window, and verified who they were. As I continued to watch the cars move along, I couldn't help thinking of the scene from *The Godfather* of the tollbooth plaza on the Jones Beach Causeway on Long Island, where I had driven hundreds of times. In the movie, Sonny Corleone drives up to one of the many tollbooths and rolls down his window to pay the toll, but instead, blocked in by cars in front of and behind him, he gets assassinated.

As I shook off my memory of the gruesome scene from *The Godfather* and looked over at Cuomo and his team, I had to smile at the circuitous path life sometimes takes. I had known Governor Cuomo for almost fifteen years. We first met in 2005, when he was running for Attorney General of New York and I was running for Lieutenant Governor. (Yes, I have had multiple careers.) We would see each other almost every week at the Democratic "chicken dinners" that were held in different counties around the state, where various candidates gathered and tried to win the Democratic committee member votes that would get them on the ballot. I think we all had memorized each other's stump speeches after three months on the campaign trail. After Cuomo won and became attorney general, I spent time with him to bring him up to speed on the healthcare issues facing both New York State and the country at large. We also saw each other frequently during a later period, when he was New York State's attorney general and I was senior adviser for Governor Paterson.

As it happened, I also had known Michael Dowling for over twenty years, because he and I had offices next to each other for six years after he became CEO of Northwell during my tenure as the first chief medical officer there. Michael is a visionary healthcare leader who has built Northwell into one of the largest, most efficient, and highest-quality health systems in the country.

"Drive-through testing is something that I hadn't heard of last week, but something we're doing this week," Cuomo said as he began to explain how the new drive-through site would work. "You *want* to find positive cases, because then you can isolate those positive cases, and find out who that person might have been in touch with. . . . The single most important thing we can do to combat and contain the novel coronavirus is to test for it."

The drive-through COVID-19 testing in New Rochelle proved to be a great success—we tested 200 people that first day and then about 500 a day from then on. Within days we had set up other drive-through sites throughout New York State, and we soon began receiving requests for special testing programs, including drive-through sites, from all kinds of clients—New Jersey and the cities of New York, Detroit, Miami, and dozens of others. Over the next six weeks BioReference became the de facto experts in drive-through testing as we opened and staffed over thirty drive-through facilities all around the country, usually in parking lots and other outdoor locations that had easy access from a major highway. We required any client that opened a drive-through to provide their own security and traffic control. This was usually the local or state police, but in some cases the state would call on the National Guard. The most pressing issue was hiring and training field staff to swab and collect specimens at the drive-throughs and then providing the logistics support to pick up those specimens and get them to the lab in a timely fashion. Early on we tested whoever showed up and had to enter their personal information on-site so that we could get their result back to them. Subsequently we developed the technology so that people could enter their information online and schedule an appointment, making the process much more efficient.

In retrospect, one of the most brilliant aspects of the drive-through model was that it addressed a largely unforeseen problem that came with COVID-19 testing and the overnight need for mass testing: It was not just the availability of COVID-19 tests and the capability to perform them that made testing so problematic during the pandemic, but it was also the basic dilemma of *where* people could go to get swabbed. Doctors' offices, hospitals, emergency rooms, urgent care centers, and lab patient service centers all were trying to keep potentially sick COVID-19 patients away from their facilities so as not to infect other patients. Large-capacity indoor facilities like auditoriums, conference centers, convention centers, hotels, and houses of worship all represented potential super-spreader venues. Drive-through sites, which kept people in their own vehicles, were safe and highly efficient. In addition, the medical staff would have only a few seconds of contact with each patient and could protect themselves by wearing masks, gloves, coverups, and face shields. The drive-through testing model proved to be, as Karen had predicted, an excellent way to test people for the highly contagious Sars-COV-2 virus. Unfortunately, despite all the advantages they offered, over time drive-through testing sites would become symbolic of the dysfunctional response of the federal government during the pandemic, as the evening news showed footage, night after night, of cars lined up for miles as people waited for hours to get a COVID-19 test. The federal government relegated testing to the states who frequently relegated the testing sites to the counties and cities. As a result, every testing venue was a separate contract negotiation without federal assistance. In some circumstances the states were able to obtain FEMA assistance at some sites, but this was the rare exception. The federal government could have developed a comprehensive national test site model supported by the National Guard, FEMA, and the public health corps to assist in staffing and traffic control, but that never happened.

Since the market abhors a vacuum, BioReference benefited from the need to tackle the logistics of drive-through testing sites on our very first day of COVID-19 testing. As we responded in real time to new challenges in New Rochelle every day, we identified and developed an important strategy that would prove invaluable not just for setting up drive-through sites, but also for setting up efficient, safe, high-volume testing in a variety of situations. That strategy was first to listen to our clients very carefully, and then to design a soup-to-nuts solution for their specific testing situation—a one-stop-shop, turnkey operation that allowed us to come in and handle every aspect of a testing operation for a client. The unfamiliar logistical and staffing challenges we encountered on that first drive-through testing site in New Rochelle forced all of us at BioReference to think outside the four walls of the lab—and outside the box.

In the case of drive-through testing, we wound up developing an all-in-one package that provided an online system for scheduling testing appointments; a barcode technology for personal cell phones that verified each patient's identity and information when they showed up to be tested; the medical staff who swabbed people while they stayed in their cars; the sequencing for bagging the specimens and transporting them to our laboratories; and the sequencing for logging in the specimens, testing the specimens and then sending the results back to both the state or local government so they could track the pandemic, and to the patients, who could go online to check their results. Remember, this was before any home kits that allowed people to self-test for COVID-19 had been developed. Our ability to set up and run these turnkey drive-through testing sites became a panacea to local and state governments, as it spared them the task of cobbling together a comprehensive solution themselves. Whoever wanted to set up drive-through testing for COVID-19 need only find the site, which usually was a very large parking lot with easy access to highways, and provide security and traffic control. We did the rest.

Crash Course #2: Meet the Press

On Saturday, March 14, the day after the press conference with Governor Cuomo in New Rochelle, my cell phone rang at 9:00 p.m. My wife Karen looked across the room at me with raised eyebrows as if to ask, "Who the hell…?" I glanced down at the phone screen. It was New York City mayor Bill de Blasio. Mayor de Blasio and I had known each other dating back to 2009 when he was on the New York City Council, and during his time as public advocate and then as mayor of NYC, and we had remained on friendly terms over the years. I was pretty sure I knew why Mayor de Blasio was calling me now, and when I answered my phone, sure enough, he wanted to know about BioReference's COVID-19 testing capabilities and whether we could divert a certain amount of our capacity to testing for New York City, as we had agreed to do for New York State. After discussing the situation with Mayor de Blasio, I agreed to discuss COVID-19 testing with the New York City Health and Hospital Corporation (NYC HHC)—the largest public healthcare system in the nation, which served more than a million New Yorkers annually in more than seventy patient care locations across the city.

Three days later, on March 17, I participated in a press conference Mayor de Blasio hosted at New York City Hall during which we announced that BioReference would be collaborating with NYC HHC to provide an additional 5,000 coronavirus tests daily. For me it was important that the expanded testing we were providing would be prioritizing New Yorkers most at risk in the epidemic, such as seniors and people with chronic health problems, with a specific focus on helping frontline physicians and healthcare providers quickly and efficiently diagnose and treat critically ill hospital patients suspected of having COVID-19 infections. As Mitchell Katz, the CEO of HHC, explained at the press conference, "Not everybody who has respiratory distress has COVID-19. Some people may be suffering from heart disease, some may have bacterial pneumonia." Determining whether or not a critically ill hospital patient was infected with COVID-19 was essential, not just so the appropriate treatments could be administered as quickly as possible, but also because any COVID-19-positive patients needed to be isolated as early as possible to avoid putting already vulnerable populations at even greater risk.

"We are in a race against time, and we are trying to rapidly make up the ground lost by the federal government in the initial weeks of this crisis," Mayor de Blasio announced. "The new partnership between HHC and BioReference means increased testing and faster results—helping save lives. . . . New Yorkers are self-reliant. New Yorkers are resourceful. This is what we do.

"We have not been sitting and crying about the fact that the federal government never really showed up," the mayor added. "Once we realized that there was an opportunity to work directly with Dr. Cohen and his company, we just went and did it. Dr. Cohen and I have had a long, wonderful relationship. I have had his cell phone for many years. I called him on his cell phone. To his great credit he immediately said, 'We want to help the people of New York City.' So here we go. It was very, very fast."

At one point in his remarks, the mayor referred to BioReference as the "cavalry who rode in to the rescue," but for me, creative collaborations between the private and public sectors in times of extreme healthcare crisis have always seemed both a duty and a privilege. As a physician, the goal of saving lives is a responsibility that I take very, very seriously. In addition to caring for the most vulnerable and at-risk people in New York City's 8.6 million population, I wanted this new collaboration with

New York City to make sure that physicians and nurses and health-care professionals on the front line, who were putting their lives at risk, would have access to testing with the quickest possible turnaround times. Launching smart public/private collaborations—and doing so quickly—was also especially critical in this instance because of the speed with which COVID-19 was spreading. Only four days prior, BioReference finally had been approved to start testing for COVID-19, and now, as I sat on a dais in City Hall before a roomful of masked journalists positioned at specified intervals in accordance with the new protocols for social distancing, some of the language ricocheting around the room was ominous. At the time of the press conference, approximately 1,000 cases of COVID-19 had been confirmed in New York City, with a total of 124 of those cases being hospitalized. But now Mayor de Blasio warned that the number of confirmed cases could balloon to 10,000 within a week. "Everything is changing very, very rapidly," he said. "We are preparing for an onslaught."

Elective surgeries already had been canceled in city hospitals, and there were plans to erect temporary medical facilities in tents around the city within the next few days. For the first time in its more than 250-year history, the annual St. Patrick's Day Parade—scheduled for that very day—had been shut down.

"You're going to see change all the time," Mayor de Blasio said. "This is a rapidly expanding crisis." Although an official order to "shelter in place" had not yet been issued, Mayor de Blasio expressed his opinion that the New York State and city governments should work together to make a decision on this matter within forty-eight hours. "We have never been here before," he said. "We are going to have to create everything from scratch."

As I sat in City Hall listening to Mayor de Blasio, I couldn't help thinking that "creating everything from scratch" was exactly what the teams in our BioReference Labs and offices were doing at that very minute. Even as the press conference ended, and the assembled crowd began to drift away, the speed at which normal life was changing made itself felt. I had taken an Uber to the press conference earlier that morning. But during the press conference, Mayor de Blasio had announced that as of that moment, as a precautionary move against further infections,

Uber services were being suspended. After making a few calls, I eventually found a ride in the back of one of the BioReference courier vans that collected COVID-19 tests from various testing sites and delivered them back to our labs. As I went bouncing down the highway with crates and crates of coronavirus-test specimens, I had to wonder what other strange and sudden changes this rapidly spreading virus might bring.

As the virus swept across the country in those first weeks, fear of infection became as contagious as the disease itself. Only two weeks earlier when I had attended the White House meeting with Vice President Mike Pence and the Coronavirus Task Force, the overall tone had basically been rah-rah—this is no big deal, we'll all work together to manage this health threat. Now the phone lines at BioReference were busy 24/7 as calls from would-be clients and media organizations from all around the country came flooding in. Natalie Cummins was answering many of those calls, and she remembers the tone of full-blown panic in the voices of those on the other end of the line as the whole country plunged into the crisis of the pandemic. She also remembers feeling an intense sense of a shared mission rise up in herself and in her colleagues as everyone in the company prepared to step up and take care of all the new emergencies that were hitting us every day.

"I remember thinking to myself this is what we do, and this is the moment that we were made for," says Natalie. "I keep notes every day, and in the second week of March in 2020 I wrote about how we were going to work with every customer that needed testing, how we would be widely accessible 24/7, how we would maintain impeccable high-quality standards and exploit our ability to be agile and develop a national footprint for COVID-19 testing. Internally, among ourselves, we were talking about all sorts of logistics like how to collect these samples, what kind of bag should they be in, what kind of labels should they have, how to pick up and transport them. Where were they going to go when they came to the laboratory? How were we going to result and report these specimens? Where were we going to store samples that we actually couldn't process immediately, because we were starting to receive so many every day?"

As the company scrambled to put together a new management structure that would address all the myriad challenges of large-scale COVID-19 testing and to staff up in order to handle the enormous numbers of specimens we were starting to collect from all over the country, I recognized the unambiguous fact that the supply chain for testing materials would become a major issue. Not only had the federal government failed to anticipate the need and create adequate stockpiles of the necessary materials for COVID-19 testing; in those early days, many hospital labs, public health labs, and regional labs had begun hoarding testing supplies. We decided to assemble a team that would deal exclusively with supply chain logistics—a problem we had never really had to worry about before.

Public interest in press interviews and TV appearances with all kinds of healthcare experts, including top executives at the big commercial diagnostic labs like myself, had increased exponentially along with public anxiety as the pandemic pushed the country into a lockdown, and this created another new and very busy front for BioReference. About six weeks earlier Hillary Titus, who had joined the company in 2018 as a product manager for our women's health team, had taken on the job as communications director. At the time she had mentioned to Natalie, to whom she reported, that she was worried that there might not be enough to keep her busy full-time, as diagnostic labs do not generally get much attention from the mainstream media. In response, Natalie had given Hillary a little pep talk, to assure her that she would have plenty to do.

"I told her, 'Hillary, we are going to *make* the news,'" remembers Natalie. "'We're going to find ways to position BioReference and the health issues that we work on.'" Eight weeks later, in mid-March with a once-in-a-century pandemic unfolding, Hillary was no longer worried about whether there would be enough for her to do. Multiple press requests were coming in everyday from mainstream and local media across the country.

"I often wondered," Hillary has since joked, "if Natalie knew something I didn't."

March 20, 2020, just three days after my New York City Hall press conference with Mayor de Blasio, was a busy media day on my early pandemic calendar. I checked in at 30 Rockefeller Plaza in Manhattan for an interview with MSNBC's *Morning Joe* show, after which I traveled to Bergen County, New Jersey, to join New Jersey governor Phil Murphy at a press conference announcing that BioReference Labs would be collaborating with the state of New Jersey to provide an additional 10,000 tests a day to residents of New Jersey. This testing would be provided through multiple drive-through sites set up by the counties around the state. LabCorp, another New Jersey–based commercial lab with revenues ten times the size of those at BioReference, was also going to be providing additional testing throughout the state, and LabCorp's senior vice president, Bill Haas, was also on the dais. At one point during the press conference, when a journalist asked about LabCorp's testing capacity, Haas replied that they could do 20,000 COVID-19 tests a day. When asked the same question, I said that BioReference could do 20,001.

As I left the press conference, I noticed a worker at a FEMA trailer packaging COVID-19 specimens. The Bergen Community College, where we had held the press conference, was a drive-through site for COVID-19 testing. Although we would provide our employees and perform testing for fifteen of the twenty-one counties in New Jersey, Bergen County was not one of them. I asked the FEMA site director, "Where are you sending the specimens?" He replied "FedEx to San Juan Capistrano, California." I knew that at that time Quest Diagnostics was performing all of their COVID-19 testing at the San Juan Capistrano facility. Prior to joining BioReference as the executive chairman, I had spent nine years as one of the five senior executives running Quest. The San Juan Capistrano facility is a terrific lab that performs highly complex testing. I had visited the facility multiple times, and I was not surprised that it would be the first lab in the Quest network to perform COVID-19 testing. But in terms of efficiency and practicality, the choice was problematic because of the location. It's just not that easy to get to the facility up in the hills of San Juan Capistrano, which could easily add significant time to any turnaround time for a test where time to result really mattered.

"Let me get this straight," I said to the FEMA director. "You are shipping these specimens to a lab 3,000 miles away, when you have BioReference five miles away and LabCorp fifteen miles away, both of which perform COVID-19 testing? You are adding at least ten hours to the turnaround time to get results."

"That's what I was told to do," the FEMA director replied. It was yet another early indicator for me that no reasonable coordination or communication existed between the federal government and the lab industry to help get efficient testing to the American public. I had weekly calls with the testing group in Vice President Pence's national task force, and no one bothered to ask me if we could provide testing for the FEMA site five miles away from us. Had no one bothered to look at a map? I didn't care that the testing was being done by Quest; I cared that those people getting tested weren't going to get their results as fast as possible. I discussed this with the testing group from the task force on our weekly call the next week in the context that we might determine some way to coordinate resource allocation between BioReference and FEMA, but this never occurred.

As I look back, the first weeks of March in 2020 seem almost surreal to me, in terms of the enormous numbers of new customers that were banging on our doors, the new complexities of what we were planning internally, and the sudden and urgent demand from the public for information about the internal workings of a laboratory—something we had not experienced often before. The March 20 New Jersey event with Governor Phil Murphy had been the third government press conference I had participated in during the one week since BioReference had received approval to conduct COVID-19 testing on March 13. Over the next twenty-four months, I would do over 150 broadcast and written press interviews as BioReference emerged as one of the leaders in the daunting challenge of how to get COVID-19 testing to people all across the country. Although we couldn't know it at the time, all of us at BioReference were just beginning what would turn out to be a two-year master class in how to quickly find solutions to difficult and unprecedented challenges, and what it takes to lead in times of crisis.

Leadership Reflection #2: Be Nice, Be Helpful, and Stay in Touch.

I have always made a concerted and consistent effort to stay in touch with the people I have encountered throughout my life and to be as helpful to them as I can, particularly when they are going through difficult times. Helping people—whether it's about finding a job, helping their child with a college application, or dealing with a medical issue in the family—not only feels good and generates a significant personal bond, but it is the right thing to do. And there is an added benefit: when you develop a network of people who feel they can count on you, you develop a network of people you can count on in return.

Having this kind of strong moral compass about helping others is one of the most important characteristics for successful leadership. My previous and current personal relationships with Governor Cuomo and Mayor de Blasio helped us successfully navigate through a complex set of issues to provide testing for the state and the city once we won the bids to provide testing. They provided us with the opportunity and trusted me that we would get it done. Michael Dowling provided Northwell medical staff to support the first drive-through while we provided testing support. We continued to collaborate with Northwell and provided them added testing resources until they could provide all of the testing needed for their hospital staff and patients. Paul Mango was instrumental in removing a regulatory obstacle that would have prevented us from providing the critical need for COVID-19 testing. Similarly, my relationships with my BioReference colleagues cultivated an atmosphere of mutual respect and loyalty, which in turn fueled a willingness in all of us to work non-stop during the pandemic and provided a sense of a shared mission that aided our success.

CHAPTER 3

Making Pancakes

On a Saturday afternoon a week after BioReference first began testing for COVID-19, I was at home watching the *PAW Patrol* cartoon with my three-year-old grandson Jackson, trying to figure out what errand I could possibly run to get out of the house. My nine-months-pregnant daughter Leslie (a microvascular plastic surgeon) was on maternity leave and had moved in with my wife, Karen, and me, along with Jackson. Her husband, Brendan, an endocrine surgeon, was taking care of COVID-19 patients at the New York Presbyterian Hospital/Weill Cornell Medical Center, where he was a full-time faculty member in the department of surgery. (Yes, if you are keeping track, there are four surgeons in the family—so far.) We had decided it was safer for Brendan to live apart from us because of his daily exposure to COVID-19 and my daughter's pregnancy. Anyone who lived with their extended family for long periods as everyone hunkered down together during the COVID-19 pandemic will understand me when I say that this cozy cohabitation can create a somewhat combustible environment. Although my son-in-law had to live alone and was exposed to critically ill COVID-19 patients on a daily basis during a time when there was no vaccine and no drug to treat the disease, I am convinced he had a better deal than me.

Mercifully, as I sat staring dully at the screen where young Paw Patrol Ryder and his rescue pups were racing around on their adventures, I was saved by the sound of my phone ringing. When I answered Dr. Robert

Redfield, the Director of the CDC, was on the line, calling to ask if I could help him with a time-sensitive issue. An eighteen-year-old patient was in the intensive care unit at JFK Medical Center in New Jersey, intubated and in critical condition from what they thought was most likely COVID-19. The attending physician wanted to place the critically ill teenager on an experimental drug, but they needed a positive COVID-19 test before they could legally put him on the experimental therapy. The hospital had no mechanism to perform a COVID-19 test. Would we be able to help? Of course, I said, and I immediately called the attending physician and we worked together to get a swab specimen from the young man delivered to our lab and tested. (For the briefest moment it did occur to me that I could go swab him myself and get out of the house for three hours—but I let that one go.) A few hours later the result for the teenager's COVID-19 test came back positive; he was placed in the experimental protocol and he survived his near-fatal brush with COVID-19.

Although the anecdote had a happy ending, for me the incident was a mind-boggling and sad testament to the disorganized state of COVID-19 testing in our country. The state of New Jersey had multiple public health laboratories and hospitals, and yet the head of the CDC for the United States of America had called me, the executive chairman of a commercial diagnostic lab, to expedite a COVID-19 test for one critically ill teenager. By now many people have heard about how the US government's failure to anticipate a need for mass testing, and the CDC's bungling of its mandate to develop and distribute a validated COVID-19 test contributed to the delay to provide adequate testing during the pandemic. But certain fundamental organizational problems within our healthcare systems also contributed to the distressing lack of COVID-19 testing in the United States. The absence of any well-organized coordination between the complicated network of diagnostic labs in this country was one big culprit. The confusing layers of federal, state, and municipal regulations that each of these labs must meet to get approval to perform any new test was another. Finally, the multiplicity of COVID-19 testing recipes that emerged during the pandemic, and the different ingredients they each required, complicated the supply chain issues exponentially.

Before COVID-19 struck, your level of interaction with or understanding of the diagnostic laboratory industry probably was limited to your annual physical, when a medical technician draws your blood or collects your urine, or your pediatrician swabs your child's throat for a strep infection. You know that the sample taken is then sent to some special place to be evaluated. Results from lab tests *are* important—in fact they are crucial to the prevention, diagnosis, and treatment of disease in 70 percent of all medical cases. But most people never even think about where that special place is or about what happens between the moment the specimen is acquired and the moment when they get their test results. Most routine blood tests that are performed in a lab are resulted within one or two days. However, complex tests like COVID-19 can usually take several days and some genetic tests can take weeks. In the early days of the COVID-19 pandemic, this changed. A speedy and accurate result from a laboratory-run COVID-19 test could mean the difference between life and death. All of a sudden, diagnostic testing moved to the forefront of people's awareness, and turnaround time became critical as they awaited the results of COVID-19 tests for themselves and their loved ones.

To help tell the full story of COVID-19 testing, I'd like to pull back the curtain and take a more detailed look both at the laboratory industry in general and at the specific problems labs experienced in the early months of COVID-19. Diagnostic testing in the United States is distributed across a complex network of public health laboratories, hospital laboratories, university laboratories, research laboratories, and for-profit commercial laboratories. States and counties across the country set up their own public health laboratories (of varying sizes) to identify and test for infectious diseases and to deal with any public health issues on a local level. In general, with any outbreak of disease the state or county Public Health Laboratories serve as the country-wide backbone for identifying and testing for infections. A few state labs, like the New York State Wadsworth Laboratory, operate as highly specialized level-three bioterrorism facilities that can detect unfamiliar and complex infectious agents. Hospital laboratories serve the patients staying in the hospital, and many also have outpatient laboratory facilities that serve their communities. University and research labs have limited testing capabilities and usually focus on a specific disease. In addition, some specialized labs perform only highly complex, infrequently ordered tests or, in some cases, only one specific test.

The commercial lab market, which does by far the bulk of medical testing in the country, is a $104 billion industry dominated by two very large commercial for-profit laboratories: Quest Diagnostics and Laboratory Corporation of America (LabCorp), with revenues of about $10 billion each. BioReference Laboratories (which serves all fifty states and has labs in New Jersey, Maryland, Florida, Texas, and California) and Sonic Laboratories, with revenues of about $1 billion each, are the next two largest national commercial laboratories. These are the four biggest commercial labs in the United States, and the rest of the commercial laboratory network is made up of hundreds of much smaller regional and local laboratories, as well as the niche specialty labs mentioned above. When you go to your physician and have your blood drawn, in most cases the blood is sent to one of these commercial labs for testing, and the result is sent electronically back to your physician. In recent years, you can now check that result online through a patient portal associated with the lab.

Exactly how things are organized inside all these laboratories can vary widely as their missions are different. Commercial labs are built to be highly efficient and profitable, with the ability to perform hundreds of thousands of tests a day. Typically, diagnostic companies, public health labs, and hospital labs are run by either nonphysician executives or by physicians trained to be pathologists. There are two major types of pathologists: anatomic pathologists, who spend their time looking through a microscope to determine if a biopsy or a certain sample of tissue is cancerous or not; and clinical pathologists, who are responsible for the operations, quality oversight, and accurate results for a laboratory that tests mostly blood or urine. I should pause here and say that in my position as executive chairman and CEO of one of the largest commercial laboratories in the country, I was an outlier. I am a vascular surgeon by training, and when I joined Quest Diagnostics, about ten years before I joined BioReference, I had almost no knowledge of the testing industry and laboratory medicine. I had been recruited by Dr. Surya Mohapatra, Quest's CEO and chairman of the board, while I was serving as the senior adviser to New York governor David Paterson. Surya is one of the smartest people I had ever met, and over ten years he increased Quest's revenues from $1 billion to $7.5 billion to make it the largest diagnostic company in the nation. He believed in me and gave me the opportunity to learn the diagnostic business, and eventually to run several of the company's largest divisions. But when I was in medical school, the idea of pathologists hard at work in laboratories did nothing for me except to conjure up a memory of a scene from the movie *Young Frankenstein*, when Igor (played by Marty Feldman) tells Dr. Frankenstein (played by Gene Wilder) that he plans to transplant the brain of someone call Aby Normal (abnormal brain) into the monster's head before they pull the switch to bring him to life. Back then Hawkeye Pierce from *M*A*S*H* was my hero, and my sole ambition was to become a surgeon. Luckily for me, when I did enter the diagnostic industry, my work never required me to go anywhere near a microscope—and the experiments conducted in both the Quest and the BioReference labs bore no resemblance to the work being done in the lab in *Young Frankenstein*.

Large commercial labs like BioReference house special machines (called analyzers or platforms, as previously noted) that can automate many of the steps for running tests on blood and urine. The robotic abilities within some of these machines, for instance, can take a tube of blood, remove the cap, remove a portion of the sample, put it onto the analyzer, run the test, report the results, and send it to the doctor and the patient via a confidential and secure online patient portal. These large automated machines have much higher throughput—the number of tests that a machine can perform in a day—than the machines in smaller labs, and the large commercial labs typically perform thousands of routine tests ordered by doctors every day. Physicians will determine which lab should test a patient specimen depending on the specific test being ordered and which laboratories are in network with a patient's health insurance. The laboratory that runs the test bills the patient's insurance for the test— sometimes the patient will have a small out-of-pocket charge, as dictated by their health insurance plan.

As I explained earlier, in 2020 when COVID-19 first hit, the official US federal plan for the outbreak of any disease was that the CDC would develop a test for the virus and then mass produce the test and send the test kits to the public health labs (but not to the commercial labs) nationwide. This had worked fairly well for previous outbreaks, including Zika,

H1N1, and avian flu as the volume of testing was easily accommodated by these public health labs. As a result, pre-COVID-19, the commercial labs had had little to do with testing during outbreaks, unless they independently decided to develop a test themselves. (As an example, when Monkey Pox broke out post-COVID-19, LabCorp decided to develop its own test independent of the CDC.) But as COVID-19 morphed from the status of "outbreak" into a full-blown pandemic, all the prior protocols and regulations determining which labs could develop and run COVID-19 tests were tossed out the window. The number of new COVID-19 cases was rising exponentially every day, and the need for mass testing had become a public health emergency. There was no way the public health labs could perform the volume of testing needed, nor were they designed to scale to develop high-throughput testing that was required. The resources of large commercial labs with machines that could run thousands of tests a day were desperately needed. On March 1, 2020, the CDC finally announced that they were going to release their test kit—also known as their "assay"—to laboratories that were interested.

When commercial labs like BioReference want to apply for approval to run a new test in their labs, they have two major models for acquiring testing capabilities. In the first, they buy a test that another company has developed—often called a "test kit," this includes all the chemicals and reagents needed to run a test along with a specific recipe explaining how to use them. Sometimes labs also will have to buy the other company's analyzer in order to run the test, and sometimes labs can run it on an analyzer that they already have. The other major model for acquiring testing capabilities is for a company to develop a test in its home lab, determining all the chemicals and reagents needed, the specific recipe for using them, and the platform or analyzer that the test will be run on. This is referred to as an LDT, or Laboratory Developed Test.

The government mishandling of COVID-19 testing has been well-documented by many, and in August 2022 CDC director Rochelle Walensky came forward and acknowledged the tragic debacle and called for an overhaul of the agency. "For 75 years, C.D.C. and public health have been preparing for COVID-19," she said, "and in our big moment, our performance did not reliably meet expectations."[2] But Walensky's 2022 admission was an understatement, given the actual events of early 2020. Not only was the COVID-19 test kit that the CDC first developed flawed in several ways, but some of the test kits the CDC sent out to other labs turned out to be worthless because they had been contaminated. Even when public health labs could get the CDC test kits to work, they did not have the throughput capacity to do mass testing. In late February 2020, when the CDC pivoted and encouraged the commercial labs to develop strategies to help test the American public for COVID-19, the activity inside our labs in Elmwood Park, New Jersey, ratcheted up to insane levels overnight. We had to make some big decisions at lightning speed. We had three options, and zero time:

1. We could develop our own test kit from scratch, creating an original recipe with the proper reagents and chemicals and analyzers (our own LDT).

2. We could use the published CDC recipe. This option would require purchasing the reagents and primers needed to run the CDC test from a company known as IDT, because it was the only manufacturer of those components at the time. And there were multiple problems with the CDC's test: in addition to not working in many labs and having been sent out contaminated in some cases, the CDC test could not be automated, and therefore was too slow to be scaled to perform high-volume testing.

3. We could purchase the tests being produced by large platform manufacturers, which would involve acquiring two major components from each manufacturer: the big, automated analyzers designed to run COVID-19 tests, and the specific reagents and chemicals—the manufacturer's own "secret sauce"—to run the tests on their big machines.

---

2   Sharon LaFraniere and Noah Weiland, "Walensky, Citing Botched Pandemic Response, Calls for CDC Reorganization," *New York Times*, August 17, 2022. nytimes.com/2022/08/17/us/politics/cdc-rochelle-walensky-covid.html.

After examining all the options, Jim Weisberger made the decision that given the urgency of the situation, we were not going to take the time and resources to develop our own COVID-19 test (LDT) from scratch. Instead, we would purchase the necessary reagents from an IDT to run the slower, more manual CDC-developed test and, at the same time, we would evaluate which platform manufacturers we should use for high-throughput testing.

"We applied for the CDC assay immediately, obviously," remembers Jim, "but it was a little tricky for a number of reasons. One was that we had to get the positive control—the viral substance itself—and the only way to do that was to apply through the CDC for some kind of a license, which could take two weeks to obtain." (As a point of interest, and as a slight aside here, the control substance for the CDC test and for all subsequent COVID-19 tests that are under Emergency Authorization Use were all derived from one person: the index case in Washington state who had traveled to China to Wuhan and come back infected. All of the probes and primers and sequences that all labs use also are derived from the viral substance from this one particular person. This has implications later on.) Jim quickly discovered that testing with the CDC assay would prove problematic for a number of other reasons as well.

"The CDC recommended an RNA extraction technique that was not scalable," says Jim. "They insisted that you had to use their particular extraction technique, which meant you could only do about two dozen tests a day." Although the CDC changed its regulations about extraction techniques after the complaints started pouring in from labs all over the country, as noted earlier, their assay was flawed in several other ways. Which is why we had decided to research several big commercial manufacturers' analyzers and test kits at the same time that we were trying to validate the CDC assay.

Each of these manufacturers, in addition to having their own analyzers and their own "secret sauce" recipes for testing, had different requirements for specimen handling, and different numbers of tests their analyzers could run in a twenty-four-hour period. The Roche platform could run 3,000 tests a day, whereas other platforms could only run several hundred a day. One machine could have results in three hours, another in six. Some of the machines were fully automated, and others required some manual preparation before specimens could be put on the analyzer. Different machines reported the results differently—some gave only a definitive positive or negative to COVID-19 being present, while others also gave numeric values that fell into an indeterminate gray zone. They each reported their results in their own way and would require different technology links into our own computer reporting systems. At the time, we had no idea how well any of them would perform.

For the first nine months of the pandemic, most COVID-19 testing was done by a process called Polymerase Chain Reaction (PCR). PCR testing for the COVID-19 virus is much more complicated than a routine blood draw and analysis. PCR testing works by repeatedly doubling any existing viral RNA present in a specimen until it has been magnified to a level where the virus becomes detectable. For example, assume you could only detect a virus when there were one hundred particles or greater of viral RNA present. If a patient's specimen has only ten particles, in the first cycle, the machine will double the number of particles to twenty particles; the second cycle will double it to forty particles; the third cycle will double it to eighty particles and the fourth cycle will double it to 160 particles. At this point the virus will be detectable (in our example, over one hundred is detectable). If, however, a patient's original specimen contains a larger amount of viral RNA, let's say fifty particles, then after only one cycle fifty becomes one hundred, and the virus is detectable. The fewer the number of cycles needed to produce a positive result for COVID-19, the higher the level of viral RNA in a patient. Conversely, the higher the number of cycles performed to get a positive result, the lower the viral RNA load.

For most of the PCR analyzers, thirty or fewer cycles to detect the virus was considered positive for COVID-19 disease, and if no virus had been detected after thirty-five cycles the specimen was considered negative for disease. Some of the analyzers did their analysis and only reported whether the patient was positive or negative, without specifying the number of cycles run to reach the result. Other analyzers, however, reported the actual number of cycles it took before a positive of negative result could be reported. On these machines, cycles between thirty and thirty-five were often indeterminate. Later on in the pandemic, for specific populations and by the request of the client, the actual number of cycles in a PCR COVID-19 test became an important issue in determining how to treat the patient.

After Jim and I and several others at BioReference turned our attention to the puzzle of which analyzers and which reagents and chemicals we should acquire, we decided to evaluate four platforms from four manufacturers: Roche, Thermo Fisher, Hologic, and Seegene. I asked Jim to meet me in the lab and walk me through the different testing options step by step for each of the four different manufacturers. We tracked each specimen from the time it arrived at the lab and reviewed what reagents and chemicals we should acquire in order to ramp up our capacity for high-volume COVID-19 testing as quickly as possible. Our choices struck me as similar to those you have when you are making pancakes.

You could dig up an old family recipe from Grandma to make pancakes from scratch using flour, sugar, milk, eggs and butter (CDC manual assay), or you can choose among dozens of brands of pancake mix in a box (purchase analyzers and recipes from manufacturing companies). Each company has its own pancake "mix" and requires slightly varying amounts of eggs, milk, and butter. The boxes come in many sizes, so each contains its own number of portions. If the pan is big enough, you can make three pancakes at once—or you can make just one pancake in a smaller pan. The time it takes to cook the pancakes varies, depending on whether you are using a gas or electric stove. Although the finished pancakes may look and taste slightly different, in the end they are all pancakes.

The question I kept asking was, which platform will get us up and running as quickly as possible and offer the greatest opportunity for achieving the goals of speed, volume, and accuracy in our new COVID-19 testing operations? We decided to lean heavily on Roche, with whom we already had a significant relationship. We had multiple manufacturing platforms in our core lab that provided us the capability to before over 3,000 different lab tests, however, we used a fair amount of Roche analyzers for highly complex testing. As it turns out, Roche had two high-throughput machines that could be used for COVID-19 testing. One could process 1,000 COVID-19 specimens a day and the other 3,000 specimens a day. Both were fully automated so required fewer steps in the overall process. We decided to add to our existing complement of Roche analyzers in different configurations in four of our five laboratories around the country that we used for COVID-19 testing. When fully functioning, these analyzers gave us the ability to perform between 30,000 and 40,000 COVID-19 specimens a day. Like everything COVID-19 related, it wasn't simple to get what we needed. We needed to obtain additional analyzers, get them installed and get the supplies needed to run the tests. Dan Zortman, senior vice president for North America, was our contact. Every commercial lab, every university lab, and every hospital lab around in the country was calling Dan to get these machines and the supplies to run the tests. In addition, Roche, a $60 billion a year company based in Switzerland, was getting requests from everywhere in the world where COVID-19 had emerged. The company could not produce the analyzers and supplies fast enough to keep up with worldwide demand. In addition, they needed their technicians to come on-site to install the machines and were constantly being called upon to repair them when they went down.

Dan and I spoke almost weekly as I pleaded, begged, cajoled, and sometimes screamed at him to get us more analyzers and the necessary supplies. I think he had an impossible job juggling the entire nation's requests as he tried to be fair and equitable in committing the limited resources. Roche became the workhorse for the country for COVID-19 testing but couldn't do it all. We performed millions of tests on the Roche analyzers during the pandemic. However, we could not depend solely on them to provide us the necessary analyzers and supplies we needed to keep up with demand. We then made what was possibly one of the most important decisions for the company during the entire pandemic. We decided that in addition to Roche, we would bring up all three of the different platforms we had evaluated, so as not to be completely dependent on one manufacturer. These three additional platforms added about 60,000 tests a day to our capacity so that we could perform about 100,000 COVID-19 tests a day if we had the supplies and the staff and all of the analyzers were running at full throttle. It took us approximately four months from when we made the decision to start testing for COVID-19 until we had the capability to perform 100,000 tests a day. We were increasing our capabilities by adding about 10,000 tests a week.

I have no problem making decisions and committing to a plan, but we were in uncharted territory staring into an unknown abyss. So, in this case, the plan became to keep all of our options open for as long as possible. We needed flexibility and the ability to pivot quickly if supplies ran short or machines broke down. Four different platforms, with thousands of different permutations relative to their reagents and chemicals and workflow and resulting. . . . All four of the platforms had to be validated and revalidated, according to which tests and swabs and reagents were being used, and all the paperwork for each had to be submitted to the appropriate authorities for official approval so that we could begin running hundreds of thousands of tests on a highly contagious virus 24/7 every day in the middle of a pandemic that had forced the country into lockdown. What could possibly go wrong?

Leadership Reflection #3: Keep Your Hand on the Pulse and Live with Uncertainty.

COVID-19 was a crisis without precedent. Operating under "fog of war" conditions, I did my best to stay abreast of emerging testing technologies and to track how the outbreak was changing, I am a voracious reader who likes to consume as much information as possible from as many sources as possible, but no matter how much information I absorbed, uncertainty remained the dominant mode. I often had to make decisions without adequate real-time data. For example, we would see spikes in COVID-19 rates in certain geographic areas over several days where we were performing the testing before it was reported in the press. We didn't know whether these spikes were going to persist but had to decide whether we would continue to devote resources to these areas of higher incidence. We would see reports of outbreaks in other areas around the country where we were not testing and had to decide whether we should scale up testing in that region without any real data as to the status of the outbreak (was it increasing or decreasing?). Later in the pandemic when we began to see decreases in testing volume, the Delta variant hit and we had to decide if we should scale back up by adding back people and supplies not knowing how long it would persist. It happened again when Omicron hit and we had already scaled back our workforce from the Delta surge. Should we scale up again without knowing the duration of the impact of the new variant? We just didn't have the data, and no one had the experience to predict what would happen.

My favorite quote from the pandemic was "COVID is where intuition goes to die." I was constantly asked what was going to happen next, and my response was always the same: "I have no idea." We all had to live with uncertainty during the pandemic, but at BioReference we continually brought our focus back to our immediate short-term plans for action, from three to six months out. We had to make some "big" calls under very stressful conditions—we made some great choices and some bad ones. Given the uncertainty of supplies to run the analyzers and how often they would require repairs, one of our good choices was to run the four different platforms and not be solely dependent on one.

CHAPTER 4

"My Kingdom for a Swab"

The moment BioReference was up and running COVID-19 tests, every imaginable subsection of society was either in discussion with us about providing testing or already sending us test specimens: states, cities, counties, hospitals, physicians, nursing homes, federally qualified health centers (FQHCs), urgent care facilities, public schools, colleges, prisons, employers of all kinds (including healthcare, food services, professional services, manufacturing, hospitality, and travel), and entertainment companies (including sports teams, movie productions, theaters, and casinos) were all banging on our door. Some of the requests we fielded during this period were quite daunting. For instance, in the late spring of 2020 the Democratic National Committee (DNC) approached us about providing a testing program for the 2020 Democratic Convention to nominate the party's candidates for president and vice president. They expected 50,000 attendees—including delegates, staff, elected officials, press, and support personnel—all of whom planned to stay in hundreds of hotels around the greater Milwaukee area. I had been to three presidential nominating conventions in the past, and I found it difficult to imagine how we would manage a situation where people entered and exited and then reentered a convention site multiple times a day without creating the greatest super-spreader event in history. At that point in the pandemic, no good point-of-care testing options had been developed, and we did not have a lab near Milwaukee that could provide quick turnaround times for test results. Thankfully, as the pandemic continued to intensify, the DNC first moved their convention date from July to August, then made the decision to downsize to about 5,000 people, and finally decided they would need to go virtual for the entire event.

The DNC's gradual realization of the serious health risks during the pandemic, particularly for large in-person events, mirrored the day-by-day learning curve everyone in the country embarked upon during those first months of COVID-19.

At BioReference, everything about how our labs and offices operated had to be redesigned overnight, and the protocols and processes continued to change week by week throughout the pandemic. In the earliest days of the COVID-19 crisis, as the country went into lockdown and many doctor's offices and hospital departments closed down, the normal incoming flow of routine medical tests slowed to a trickle in our labs, and we were forced to furlough many of our employees. With the sudden and urgent need for COVID-19 testing all across the country, we had to pivot and try to bring back our furloughed people as well as hire as many new people as possible. This was not an easy process; the general public's fear of contracting the virus was intense, and many of the people we sought to interview would hang up the moment they heard the work involved COVID-19 testing. Even among our seasoned laboratorians, who were used to wearing full PPE and who had been specifically trained to handle various (sometimes quite nasty) specimens, the mood was jittery. Nobody really knew what this new virus was or how it spread—and lots of people were dying from it. When someone in the production line for running tests sneezed or coughed, nervous voices would call out from down the line: "I can't take it home . . . I have an elderly, immune-compromised family member!"

Everyone involved in healthcare had to face new and unpredictable challenges in those first months of COVID-19 —both at work and at home, where families had to deal not only with the sense of uncertainty and fear that hung like a dark cloud over everything, but also with food shortages, restless children who were out of school, and other pandemic-induced hardships. From the moment we began testing for COVID-19 at BioReference, everyone labored with an unstoppable, fierce effort to expand our daily testing capacity—a process that put pressure on every single department. Although we had a network of five laboratories—in New Jersey, Maryland, Florida, Texas, and California—none had done COVID-19 testing before, and two of the five had never performed any highly complex molecular PCR-type testing. All our labs had to be redesigned to handle the various stages of COVID-19 testing and refitted with all kinds of special equipment, from analyzers to freezers to computers to dashboards that kept track of operations. Warehouses had to be overhauled, courier vans rented, newly hired staff trained, IT systems redesigned. We started out with a capacity for running several hundred tests a day, and we peaked at a capacity to perform 100,000 tests a day. Throughout this time, we never knew where any of it was going or where we would land. No one knew how long the pandemic would last.

During these early months of the pandemic one of the greatest frustrations for all of us at BioReference—and one we had to deal with every day—was the fact that we couldn't increase the number of people tested for COVID-19 because we couldn't get the supplies needed to run the tests. As I mentioned earlier, the federal government had never anticipated an outbreak in which it would be necessary to run hundreds of thousands if not millions of tests a day, and as a result, it had neither stockpiled the supplies required nor made a plan for how to distribute those supplies in order to administer testing on a massive scale. The tragic result was that as COVID-19 swept across the nation, the supply chains for nearly every aspect of a COVID-19 test—the analyzers to run the tests, the chemical reagents to run on the analyzers, the plastic pipette tips to measure specimens, the personal protective equipment for workers, the plexiglass to set up safe shielded areas and, perhaps most crucial of all, the swabs and the fluid to transport the swab specimens to the lab—were all scarce or just plain nonexistent.

The Supply Chain Dilemma

Every real-time reverse transcription polymerase chain reaction COVID-19 test—the gold standard of COVID-19 tests—begins with the mighty swab. A patient gets swabbed, the swab is placed into a tube with a fluid, known as transport medium, and the combination of the swab and the tube of fluid—frequently referred to as the "test kit"—is sent to the lab.

This was why, when it came to supply chain problems, the swab shortage was particularly egregious and frustrating: you couldn't start the testing process unless you could get a specimen, and you couldn't get a specimen without a swab. If it hadn't been such a sad situation, in which people's lives were literally at stake, the degree to which swabs became the "coin of the realm" might have been comical. After all, it would seem that a simple ball of cotton (or in most cases polyester) stuck on the tip of a plastic stick, an item which costs about thirteen cents, would be ridiculously easy to manufacture and distribute. But like everything related to COVID-19, it just wasn't that straightforward.

Swabs are made from different materials, that are specific to the type of specimen to be acquired. In order to ensure accurate test results, the specific type of swab used to collect any given specimen must be combined with a specific type of reagent, all of which can vary depending on which type of analyzer, or platform, the test will be run on. To further complicate matters, the type of medium used to transport the swab from the test site to the lab also can affect the results. The four platforms we were running each had different nuances and requirements in terms of getting a validated result. The permutations and combinations of recipes that would be needed were endless. Jim Weisberger had to run hundreds and hundreds of experiments to validate that a particular combination of swab type, transport medium type, reagent type, and analyzer model would produce clinically accurate and relevant results.

Even the question of how to brandish the mighty swab properly for the purposes of COVID-19 testing seemed to be a complicated issue. At the beginning of the pandemic, people had to undergo nasopharyngeal swabbing, an unpleasant experience that feels like the swab is going up into your brain. (In fact, if performed improperly it can do just that, puncturing the membrane between the nasal passage and the brain.) Next, the approved technique moved to what is called mid-turbinate swabbing, which went halfway up your nose, and then eventually to lower nasal swabbing, a procedure which is extremely well tolerated. Some people underwent pharyngeal swab, whereby the specimen was obtained by placing the swab directly into the back of the throat, a procedure that frequently caused patients to gag and cough onto the unfortunate examiner. We decided not to train our staff to conduct throat swabs because many people found it so uncomfortable to have their throat swabbed. I do not mean to imply that we stuck with nasal swabbing because it was easier. Some nasal swab specimens from patients with severe upper respiratory symptoms came in with so much thick mucus in the test kit that we couldn't run them. The "snot," as Jim very scientifically dubbed the gummy substance, was so thick he had to devise special procedures for running these specimens on the analyzer without clogging up the entire machine. We also made the decision not to use saliva as a specimen type, whereby patients would "spit" into a different type of tube, because we had redesigned our labs for large-scale testing on nasal swab samples and we didn't want to lose time validating another specimen type and undergoing another redesign.

But by far the biggest problem with nasal swabbing for COVID-19 tests was the shortage of swabs, and the biggest reason for the shortage was that there were only two companies manufacturing swabs: Copan Diagnostics in Italy, and the US-based Puritan Medical Products, located in the tiny hamlet of Guilford (population 1,500) in Piscataquis County in the state of Maine. Over the years this small family-owned business, which started in 1919 as a producer of mint toothpicks, had gone on to produce popsicle sticks and tongue depressors until finally landing upon swabs as its specialty. Modestly billed on the home page of its website as "America's Swab Experts," the company makes sixty-five varieties of swabs, three of which—foam, spun polyester, and flock—are used for coronavirus testing.[3] In early 2020, as the pandemic spread exponentially and testing supplies were running short, the US government called Puritan with a desperate plea for swabs and offered government financing for Puritan to increase its production. Around this time the government also arranged to have military planes fly to Italy to bring back shipments of swabs—on April 3, 2020, it was reported that seven C-19 military planes had transported 3.5 million swabs from Italy to the United States. In the meantime, Puritan Medical Products had begun building additional facilities and staffing up to increase its swab production. By

---

3   Karen Heller, "It's the Golden Age of the Swab, a 99-Year-Old Invention That Has Never Been More Crucial," *Washington Post*, January 10, 2022. washingtonpost.com /lifestyle/2022/01/10/swab-test-covid-puritan-medical/.

2022, Puritan's production was up from the 5 million swabs a month that it was producing in the early pandemic, to 300 million swabs a month. But back in March and April 2020, the scarcity of swabs was such a critical problem that many of us in the diagnostic industry became semi-obsessed with the little cotton- or polyester-topped sticks.

Our supply chain staff worked eighteen-hour days, seven days a week, to procure as many swabs as possible. We would then distribute the precious items to our clients through a carefully monitored distribution system designed to prevent clients and field representatives from hoarding supplies. If we sent a client 200 swabs, we would not send them any more until we had received 200 COVID-19 tests back from them. Our supply chain staff had to negotiate with a network of suppliers every day, begging and borrowing whatever they could. It was literally like a back-alley black-market situation—"I know a guy who knows a guy who can get several thousand swabs from China." We often didn't know who we could trust to actually deliver the goods, or what the quality of the products would be. Sometimes we had to resort to horse-trading tactics, exchanging reagents or PPE gear for swabs. We had visions of boxes of swabs conveniently falling off the backs of trucks and then being sold on the swab black market. At times we felt like actors in a bad gangster movie.

During this period the COVID-19 testing world experienced a number of unfortunate supply chain fiascos—one lab improvised with its combinations of reagents and analyzers and inadvertently used a combination that produced cyanide gas. Fortunately, no one was hurt. In another fiasco, a huge shipment of several thousands of PPE gowns imported from China proved to be substandard and useless as protective gear. When we were hit with shortages of transport fluid, we set up shop and started manufacturing it ourselves, and eventually put together our own "swab test kits" for distribution. But by far the most frustrating supply chain issue was always, hands down, the shortage of swabs. Our negotiations with a potential new client—such as a county in which we were going to set up and run a drive-through testing site—depended on whether or not we could provide COVID-19 test kits. If we couldn't provide the swabs, then there was no deal. At one point we tried our hand at 3D printing to make swabs, and at another we experimented with repurposing vaginal swabs used to test for sexually transmitted diseases as nasal swabs. When a friend of mine's wife was tested for COVID-19 with one of these repurposed swabs, I told him the good news was she was negative for COVID-19, but the bad news was she was positive for syphilis. He didn't think my joke was so funny. One of my passions is contemporary art, both painting and sculpturing, and when I created a sculpture of a woman's head with hair that resembled cotton swabs and dubbed her Swabitha, my colleagues didn't think that was too funny either. I liked to have Swabitha displayed in splendor on my desk—a sculptural ode to the perils of the pandemic—but when we had group meetings in my office people would sometimes find Swabitha's stare too intense and would request that she be sequestered.

It still astounds me that during these difficult times, when critical supplies were so scarce, we never once received any assistance from the federal government. By this time, BioReference had emerged as one of the leading COVID-19 testing labs in the nation, processing 80,000 tests a day with a forty-eight-hour turnaround time. But despite begging the Testing Diagnostic Work Group of the White House Coronavirus Task Force for more swabs almost every week, we never received any help.

The Prickly Question of Priority—Who Gets Tested First?

Two other important matters came to the forefront because of the mismatch between supply and demand for COVID-19 testing. One was the sensitive issue of priority—when there were not enough supplies and tests to go around, who should be tested first? No government agency offered any official guidance or even generally accepted rationale for how to decide who should jump to the front of the line for speedy testing and results. This was a critical issue for me, particularly when it came to ICU patients and healthcare workers, who have always been at the top of my priority list. During my six years of training to be a vascular surgeon, which included five years of general surgery and one year of specialized vascular surgery, I spent a significant amount of time in intensive care units taking care of critically ill patients. While practicing as a vascular surgeon, many of my patients needed to spend the first twenty-four to forty-eight postoperative hours in the intensive care unit. These experiences had helped shape my great respect for the nursing staff, physicians, and affiliate healthcare workers who worked in the ICU. These indefatigable folks work tirelessly in a grueling and strenuous environment where critical decisions have to be made minute to minute. With the outbreak of the COVID-19 pandemic, as everyone had to work using personal protective equipment to help prevent them from getting the disease, the already stressful work environment of the ICU became even more intense.

As the number of critically ill climbed, and death became more and more prominent, the emotional stress that piled up on top of all the physical challenges these frontline healthcare workers had to endure was horrifying. Anything that the company could do to provide speedy testing for these heroes, as well as certain other high-risk individuals, became our first and foremost priority. The rules I established for BioReference were that ICU patients, hospital patients, healthcare workers, and frontline emergency workers such as police and firefighters were to go to the front of the line. We used a color-coded system in the field, where we affixed purple labels to the samples with the highest priority, making those specimens easily identifiable when they arrived at the lab, where they were moved to the front of the line to be processed as quickly as possible. We were the first laboratory in the country to set up such a priority system.

When specimens came in, they were placed in "bins" in the refrigerators, organized by the date they were received. Each bin could have as many as a thousand samples and, unfortunately, we did not have a barcode tracking system for specimens once they had arrived in the lab. Once a specimen arrived in the lab, it was nearly impossible to find until it had gone through the entire process of being accessioned and then tested. And yet, I received calls almost every day from people I knew, looking for their result or requesting that it get tested as soon as possible. "I need to visit my family," "I need to get on a plane," "My daughter is not feeling well"—on and on went the requests. On occasions when I asked one of the techs to go find a specific specimen and load it onto the analyzer for one of the next runs, he or she would have to sort through thousands of specimens to find it.

During press interviews I was frequently challenged about how we made decisions as to who received priority testing, especially once we started testing for sports teams. My answer was always the same: "ICU patients, health care workers, and first responders come first, otherwise there is no priority." With no CDC guidance, we were in no position to decide who was more important: The general public? A nursing home patient, a teacher, an elected official, an employee working at a grocery store? We couldn't possibly say.

The Tyranny of Turnaround Time

The third issue exacerbated by inadequate supplies for COVID-19 testing was the so-called turnaround time (TAT). In normal times, turnaround time referred to the time a specimen arrived at the lab until the time the result was reported back to the client, a span that could vary according to the type of test. But COVID-19 test results were fraught with far greater concern than the results of normal blood or urine tests. A positive COVID-19 test result meant a patient had a highly infectious, potentially fatal disease; it meant the patient should self-isolate to prevent the spread of the disease, and they ought to consider and inform anyone who they might have exposed to the disease. Later, when treatments became available, it also meant that the infected patient would need to weigh the pros and cons of seeking treatment. With the increasing demand for speedy results for COVID-19 tests, the general public's focus on the turnaround time at the lab became intense, and many of our clients began to measure turnaround time as the span from the moment a swab specimen was taken to the moment they received a test result (i.e., including any transport time to the lab). Most of these clients didn't realize that the entire sequence for COVID-19 testing, from collecting a specimen at a test site to reporting the results, involved multiple steps that could significantly impact turnaround time—especially in spring 2020, when many steps that eventually became automated were still executed manually.

In the early months of the pandemic, every swab specimen went through at least seven major steps:

> **Step 1.** The patient shows up to get tested and fills out a requisition with five to ten pieces of relevant information including name, date of birth, health insurance etc.

Step 2. The patient gets swabbed, and the swab is placed into a small tube with fluid, called transport medium. The patient's name and date of birth are written onto the tube, the tube is placed into a bag with the requisition and sealed.

Step 3. The specimen is transported to the laboratory—by car, truck or plane via a lab courier, or by FedEx.

Step 4. Upon arrival at the laboratory, the requisition is removed from the bag and the patient's information is entered manually into the computer systems which then prints a label with a barcode containing the information. This label is affixed to the patient's tube.

Step 5. The tube is brought to the laboratory where a technician unseals it under a hood and transfers (using a plastic tube called a pipette) a certain amount of the fluid onto special plates, to make the viral RNA available for extraction—an automated process for some analyzers and a manual process for others. Later in the pandemic, manufacturers developed special robotic extractors to speed up the process.

Step 6. The extracted RNA is placed onto the PCR analyzers and run through the PCR process.

Step 7. Results go directly from the analyzers into our lab computer system, which forwards them to several recipients: the state or some other government agency, the ordering entity (the medical person at a company responsible for oversight of the results), the patient's portal (so people could review their result), and the ordering physician's medical records database. We had to custom build each of these online connections for each new client.

These were the basic steps for conducting COVID-19 PCR testing, but there were so many other factors that could affect turnaround time that were beyond our control. Such as:

1. Supplies to run the tests.
2. Availability of staff. All told, we wound up doubling our staff, from 4,000 to 8,000—an interviewing and hiring process that had its own unpredictable ebb and flow.

3. Temperamental machine performance. Many of the analyzers performed at only 70 percent efficiency, because 30 percent of the time they were broken down and in need of maintenance or new parts. Frequently, highly trained technicians from an analyzer's manufacturer would need to come and repair the machine on-site.
4. Transportation of the specimens often varied with weather conditions, as well as vehicle and staff availability.
5. Finally, and perhaps most important, we had zero control over (and no way to predict) the volume of specimens coming into the lab every day which could vary by as much as 30,000 specimens from day to day.

Although we developed sophisticated models to predict how many tests we could perform day to day based on the supplies we had on hand, the volume of specimens we estimated would be coming from our larger clients, the availability of staff and the state of our machines' performance, we had no way to control the overall daily volume. As a result, our ability to turn around results within forty-eight hours varied from day to day. For example, if we determined that we could perform 80,000 tests on a Monday but 120,000 specimens arrived instead, it immediately put us 40,000 behind going into the Tuesday. If 120,000 arrived again on Tuesday, we would be 80,000 behind by Wednesday. By Thursday a backlog of patients would have had to await results for three or four days. Many of our clients, such as physician groups and our Rite Aid and CVS partners who were testing the general public, could not predict the number of patients who would show up for tests either. I am a huge fan of *The Wizard of Oz*, and I have a crystal ball that sits on a small conference table in my office. Every couple of days someone would ask me jokingly if I could look into the crystal ball and tell them what the COVID-19 volume would be for the next several days, since our predictive mathematical models were so unreliable. My frequent snarky response was that my senior staff reminded me of characters from the movie: Scarecrow (you need a brain), Lion (get some courage), Tin Man (you have no heart), Glinda (good witch), and the Wicked Witch. One day when we were experiencing particularly bad problems relative to supplies in the field, shortage of staff, and delays in results, one of our executives plopped herself down at the meeting and said she was having a total "meltdown." Never being one to miss an opportunity to make fun of someone, I drew a picture on her whiteboard in her office of a puddle of water with a black hat and a broom depicting the "meltdown" of the wicked Witch after Dorothy poured water on her. She refused to erase it, and the drawing remained on her whiteboard for over two years during the pandemic. Of course, my fellow executives referred to me as either the Wizard with no power to actually make anything happen or as Dorothy leading them down a Yellow Brick Road to nowhere.

For the most part, the American public had no knowledge of these backstage laboratory issues. They only knew that sometimes they had to sit in their cars for hours waiting to be tested at a drive-through site, only to have to wait up to fourteen days for some lab to send them their result. In general, the press coverage of the testing industry was brutal during this time. The media often blamed the labs for not delivering timely results but never reported much about the challenges we encountered. On many occasions I wished I could click my heels three times and make everything go back to normal.

Our teams at BioReference did an amazing job of managing the backlog of incoming tests that could create long turnaround times—a situation we sometimes referred to as "creep." But by the end of June 2020, we could not get ahead of the curve. Within one week, our turn-around time went from forty-eight hours to five days. In addition to the negative impact on patients, we faced a reputational risk. We had been holding ourselves up as the lab with the shortest reliable turnaround time, and we did not want to hurt that reputation. We had to find a way to get control of the situation.

Throughout the pandemic the senior executive staff at BioReference, including the president (Geoff), the chief operating officer (Craig), the chief commercial officer (Natalie), chief legal officer (Jane), the chief compliance officer (Rob), the chief information officer (David), the chief digital officer (Richard), the SVP of advanced diagnostics (Ellen), the SVP of strategic ventures (Cindy), the SVP of human resources (Greg), the chief financial officer (Kevin), and the communications director (Hillary), met in person with me at least once a week, in addition to having multiple conference calls every day to address the endless ongoing COVID-19 issues. On the Thursday before the July 4th weekend, Geoff Monk, a classic operations executive whom I had appointed as president when I first arrived at BioReference in 2019, looked at the data on the screen in our executive meeting and said: "We have to think about shutting down the lab. Otherwise, there's probably no way we will ever get back to our forty-eight-hour turnaround time." Just as Jim Weisberger knew everything about how the clinical lab functioned from a scientific point of view, Geoff knew everything about how to run the operational aspects of the laboratory, from specimen acquisition through reporting results. An engineer by background, he was process-focused and data-driven when it came to making decisions. From the earliest days of the pandemic, he had been reorganizing and restructuring our COVID-19 operations for maximum efficiency and gathering the metrics—including metrics for each analyzer—that would allow us to evaluate how we were performing every day.

Geoff's suggestion that we shut down the lab would be a huge decision for us to make. With the exception of the highest priority patients and health workers, who would be exempted, we would have to notify every one of our hundreds and hundreds of clients that for seventy-two hours, we would accept no specimens. It was an unprecedented—and not inexpensive—move to make. In addition to the immediate loss of revenue, there was the potential loss of clients who would be angry with us for shutting down. But the analysis was clear: we would never get back to where we wanted to be unless we stopped testing, regrouped, and recaptured our ability to execute forty-eight-hour turnaround times.

Given the potential implications of this decision, I wanted to make sure that the leadership of OPKO, the parent company and owner of BioReference, was on board with the decision. Dr. Phillip Frost is the CEO and chairman of OPKO, the publicly traded bio-pharma and diagnostics company that had purchased BioReference in 2015. Phil is a brilliant self-made physician executive, entrepreneur, investor, inventor, and philanthropist. Phil and I spoke almost every day about a multitude of issues, and he always expressed his opinion. But to his credit, he rarely interfered with any decision I made relative to BioReference. In this case, I wanted to make sure he was on board with the decision to close the lab for three days, which would mean the loss of several million dollars. Phil never flinched; he agreed with and fully supported our decision.

We had made the decision to shut down the lab for seventy-two hours, to catch up on the existing backlog, to add capacity, to be transparent with our clients and to hope they did not bolt. In the end, we were rewarded. We did not lose a single a client, and the added capacity and throughput quickly made up for the temporary loss of revenue. Within three days, we were back on track with our forty-eight-hour turnaround time. And as it turned out, our decision to shut down and the way we navigated through the situation became the focus of an extensive and very positive article published in the *Wall Street Journal* on September 6, 2020, titled: "Labs Struggle with Surge in COVID Testing Demand; How One Made It Through."

Leadership Reflection #4: Protect Your Reputation Regardless of Costs.

Reputation is one of the most important issues—if not *the* most important issue—for every person or company. Once a reputation has been damaged, it is almost impossible to recover. With companies, it is often their response to some unexpected crisis that winds up defining them in the future. History is full of examples of how poor responses to crises have killed companies, frequently because during the crisis, the potential financial and legal repercussions of making the right decision crept in and clouded the judgement of those in charge. In the case of our laboratory shutdown, we knew the decision would cost us several million dollars and we would irritate hundreds of clients, thereby running the risk of losing them to other testing vendors. However, our reputation as the company continuously working to maintain a forty-eight-hour turnaround time and always prioritizing those in the greatest danger was at stake, and what mattered most was that we remain true to our commitments. The decision was the right one, and because we were transparent and took the time to communicate with our clients beforehand, all of them stuck with us.

CHAPTER 5

Teamwork for a Slam Dunk in the NBA Bubble

One of the biggest milestones in terms of national awareness that the COVID-19 pandemic was ushering in a whole new ballgame, so to speak, came on March 11, 2020, when the National Basketball Association (NBA) announced that a player on the Utah Jazz, which later came to be known was center Rudy Gobert, had tested positive for the virus, and that as a result the NBA was suspending its season. The day had begun with San Francisco's Golden State Warriors announcing that they would be playing a home game without fans present because of the virus—a stunning statement in itself—and now came the unthinkable news that the entire NBA season would be suspended. Mark Cuban, the owner of the Dallas Mavericks, spoke for much of the country when he expressed his shock that same day in an interview with ESPN during a game between the Mavericks and the Denver Nuggets.

"This is crazy. This can't be true," Cuban said. "This seems more out of a movie than reality." Indeed, for many the suspension of the NBA season was alarming proof that the virus was going to disrupt life in truly unfortunate and unforeseeable ways. Oh my God, they've actually suspended the basketball season? What on earth would come next?

On April 8, less than a month after the suspension of the NBA season, the NBA called BioReference's offices to initiate discussions about possible strategies for reopening the season if it became appropriate to use testing to help do so. From the beginning of our discussions the NBA expressed their commitment to using the most sophisticated science available to keep their players and staff as safe as possible. They had hired several well-known experts to help them navigate through the pandemic, had been speaking with dozens of testing manufacturers and other labs to see which could provide the best solution, and they wanted to be fully involved in the execution of whatever testing program was eventually recommended. As time progressed, they decided to try to set up a single site model where testing could help a return to play. They were seriously considering the ESPN *Wide World of Sports* center on the Disney campus in Orlando, Florida, as their location. Their hope was that if they maintained strict control of access to a self-contained campus and instituted vigorous COVID-19 testing rules, they could attempt to prevent any spread of the virus and conclude the 2019–2020 NBA season that had been halted in March. They had been researching what it would take to set up their own lab on the Disney site, but when they learned that BioReference had a fully equipped large commercial diagnostic lab in Melbourne, Florida, only seventy-two miles from Orlando, with the Roche analyzers that their experts had recommended, they turned to us instead. Early in the pandemic we had several clients who asked for advice about setting up their own COVID-19 testing lab, but once they realized how difficult this would be they almost all rejected the idea. One exception was Jeff Bezos's Amazon company, which consulted with us at length about setting up testing programs, and then decided to build their own lab to test employees during the pandemic.

I knew that designing and running the COVID-19 testing and screening programs the NBA was proposing would be both an unprecedented and a hugely ambitious challenge. After thinking about who could act quickly to organize the teams and figure out how to get the job done, I turned to Natalie Cummins, our senior vice president and chief commercial officer, and asked her to be our senior point person for the NBA. Natalie is a veteran of the diagnostic industry, and what I like to refer to as a strong utility player. She had joined BioReference in 2018, and prior to COVID-19 she oversaw the divisions that handled the sales and servicing of our commercial accounts and our health insurance plans, as well as the marketing and communications for the entire company. Natalie had taken part in the negotiations for and operation of all of our new COVID-19-related contracts thus far, and I knew that I could put her in front of any client as the senior representative for the company and she would do a great job. Sure enough, Natalie quickly put together a talented team to tackle the unique challenges of the NBA contract. Over the next few months Natalie and her team had a series of intensive discussions with David Weiss, the NBA's SVP for player matters; Dr. John DiFiori, NBA director of sports medicine; and Dr. Leroy Sims, NBA head of medical affairs. Together they hammered out the logistics for setting up and running the operation that would become famous across the country as the "NBA Bubble."

During those initial discussions with the NBA, as I began to think strategically about opportunities for COVID-19 testing in the world of sports in general, I enlisted the help of a BioReference employee who had substantial experience in sports-related laboratory testing—David Steinfeld. David had worked with me at Quest on a testing program for professional athletes called "Blue Print for Athletes," which was a comprehensive wellness program designed for professional athletes. He had developed an extensive network of contacts within the sports world and became our secret weapon. Through his contacts we soon launched discussions about COVID-19 testing with several other sports entities, including Major League Soccer (MLS), Major League Baseball (MLB), the National Hockey League, and the National Football League (NFL).

As plans for the NBA's Bubble moved forward, the NBA negotiated with Disney to create a closed campus using several buildings on the Walt Disney World resort and to use the ESPN *Wide World of Sports* facility for its games. The MLS meanwhile had contracted to share space on the Disney campus, and by June 2020 BioReference was beginning to conduct COVID-19 testing in the Orlando Disney Bubble for both NBA staff members and for members of the MLS, though the two campuses remained independent of each other and did not overlap. The NBA players were due to arrive in July 2020. To get the Bubble launched, our teams worked closely with the NBA to design the on-site logistics and hire staff for every aspect of COVID-19 testing—scheduling, accessioning, swabbing, delivering specimens to the lab in Melbourne, reporting results within a specified time frame, ordering and managing supplies, designing and maintaining safe testing areas, and operating various mobile test sites in vans around the Disney campus, to name just a few. But for us a new and steep challenge came when the NBA decided that in addition to having team players and everyone on staff undergo a PCR lab test each day, they wanted us to be able to support the capacity for everyone to have point-of-care (POC) rapid tests, if necessary. Although we were a large commercial diagnostic lab with extensive experience running thousands of lab tests every day, we had never been in the point-of-care business before. Traditionally, most point-of-care devices were set up in physician offices to run tests for glucose levels, blood count and the seasonal flu. These devices were manufactured independently, sold by distributers and run by the physician's office staff. But those manufacturers and distributers had essentially nothing to do with the new and constantly evolving COVID-19 point-of-care devices, which were part of an underdeveloped and chaotic market at the time.

During a pandemic there are several phases of testing that *should* occur. First, the CDC is supposed to develop a test that can be rolled out to the public health labs around the country (as we have seen, this was botched by the CDC). Second, if mass testing is needed, the platform manufacturers should develop testing capabilities on their high-throughput analyzers so that hundreds of thousands of people can be tested each day. (The United States had no plan for this.) Third, rapid point-of-care testing should be developed to facilitate people getting tested quickly on-site in different locations, such as in doctor's offices or clinics. (The United States had no plan for this.) Finally, at-home test kits that people can conduct on themselves, similar to pregnancy tests, should be readily available to make it as easy as possible for people to get tested whenever and as often as they may need. (The United States had no plan for this.)

Although the market had begun to respond to the need for rapid COVID-19 POC testing, the federal response to the pandemic had not included any regulations or oversight rules for this kind of testing, nor had it addressed the issues of how and where people would be able to get access to rapid testing. The overall lack of knowledge about and access to COVID-19 POC testing was compounded by the fact that in those early days of the pandemic, when dread of contagion was intense, facilities like physician offices, clinics, and emergency rooms that had some prior experience with POC testing for routine medical issues, did not want people who might have COVID-19 coming into their facilities, and therefore they did not offer COVID-19 POC testing.

For BioReference, providing POC testing for the NBA meant launching the company and its resources into totally uncharted territory. We were used to conducting highly complex tests in our clinical labs under the strictest regulatory lab standards—but now we were talking about testing in a what would essentially be a CLIA-waived setting (a lab site that is exempt from the Clinical Laboratory Improvement Amendments certificate required for most diagnostic lab testing) in various rooms through several hotels on the NBA's campus. Not only was this completely new terrain for us, but we were on an extremely tight deadline to get everything figured out and running smoothly by July 2020 when the basketball players were scheduled to arrive in the Bubble.

To set up POC testing sites we would have to address multiple new and unfamiliar issues:

1. What were the local requirements for a POC testing site? We needed approval to run a CLIA-waived testing site, where the normal laboratory oversight regulations would not apply, but other state regulations relative to rapid POC testing would apply. These regulations vary from state to state.

2. How would we evaluate the performance of different devices in the immature but burgeoning field of COVID-19 POC testing analyzers? Which technology would be best for the particular application vis-à-vis the NBA?

3. How would we report the results to the state, the patient, and the client from the testing site? In this case, we would need to report to Florida, the individual NBA players and staff, and the NBA itself.

4. What would we do about physician oversight? Every test needed to be ordered by a physician, and every test result had to be reviewed by a physician.

5. How would we register patients on-site, and what information would we require?

6. How many people could we test in what time frame at each site?

7. How would we maintain quality control in the field? We were determined to maintain BioReference's high standards of scientific accuracy, safety, efficiency, and transparency on all fronts at all times.

8. What kind of personnel did we need for the various stages of running POC tests on hundreds of people every day, and how were they to get trained to perform the testing on-site?

As it turned out, once again the answer to all these questions lay in assembling the right team of individuals and turning them loose. Natalie grabbed Mohit Mathur, PhD, vice president of medical affairs at BioReference, who had been focusing primarily on a flagship product for prostate cancer called 4Kscore, and pulled him over to work full-time on developing protocols in the NBA Bubble, for both lab-based and POC tests. For Mohit this involved not only choosing and validating the POC analyzers we would use (we started with Sophias, then worked at the NBA's request to move to PCR and piloted the use of Accula and Cue machines—more on this in chapter 9), but also hiring staff and setting up programs to train people to swab patients, run the devices, and enter the results into a database. All of this data had to be sent to our existing reporting systems back in New Jersey and then reported to the State databases and to the Department of Health within a specified time frame. None of this technology existed, and we needed to develop standard operating procedures to make sure we were consistent in how we applied the technology for different analyzers in different venues. Every testing site required certification, which involved verifying certain conditions in terms of temperature and humidity among other things and, as mentioned, every test required an ordering physician. I can't possibly overstate the Herculean task it was to pull this off. We weren't just building the plane as we flew it, we were flying blind with no compass and no outside help.

With intense coordination between quality systems, IT, marketing, sales and almost every other division of the company, we managed to set up fifteen test sites for the NBA Bubble in different resorts on the Disney property and some surrounding hotels. Rachel Moye, who had more than twenty years of experience in the lab business and who had come to BioReference in May 2020, was the powerhouse who managed the BioReference staff of more than 400 employees who worked in or near the Bubble. (Like many other people who had worked with me at Quest, Rachel had migrated to BioReference after I became CEO there.) I knew that if I asked Rachel to get something done, she would make it happen. Rachel remembers working seventeen hours a day seven days a week—including calls (at least) twice daily and at any hour with the NBA—under highly stressful conditions during the launch the NBA Bubble. On a typical day the staff for the first shift would report to work at 5:00 a.m. for a team huddle and daily reminders about important protocol issues such as confidentiality, wearing your PPE at all times, and making sure you're cleaning your pens by wiping them with disinfectant. At 6:00 a.m. the testing rooms opened. The NBA had designated times and locations for each team to come in for testing: the players and the coaches would come together at their designated time and place, and then the other league staff would come at different designated times and locations. For any vendors working in the Bubble, there was also daily testing, usually swabbed at a special trailer testing site which was open all day. Ironically, the device that ended up being used for individual identification for testing was the Disney Magic Band—an electronic wrist bracelet that people used in normal times to access different entertainment areas of the resort. Every individual's band ran through an NBA data hub and hooked directly into our IT systems for accessioning at the testing sites for easy wrist swipe check in. Between every accessioning appointment and every specimen collection, cleaning staff would come in and wipe everything down with disinfectant. Couriers left every two hours all day, to deliver PCR test specimens to the Melbourne lab.

In addition to the intense pressure of processing thousands of COVID-19 tests a day and dealing with unexpected machinery breakdowns and staffing crises, our teams had to deal with a number of sensitive issues peculiar to the Bubble itself. Security was very strict in terms of who could actually enter the Bubble and who had access to certain specific areas within the Bubble.

The NBA had stringent rules about any interaction with players. Although BioReference staff working within the Bubble were tested daily, because BioReference employees lived outside the Bubble and commuted in daily, they were not allowed to ride in the same elevators with players or team staff, and they had to eat their meals in their own designated dining space. The NBA stipulated strict rules which forbade any fraternizing with the players, or any mention of them on social media. For the most part our BioReference staff respected these codes of conduct, but basketball players are superheroes to many of their fans, and on a few occasions people violated the ground rules, and we had to let them go.

For everyone working in our Melbourne, Florida, lab seventy-two miles away from the Disney Resort, the NBA Bubble experience was intense. Eva McCoy was Rachel Moye's counterpart in the Melbourne lab, where she oversaw a staff of 171 and a brood of high-throughput analyzers that she knew so intimately she had a pet name for each one. Eva, who has been in the lab business for over thirty-nine years, remembers being on vacation at a seafood festival in the Florida Keys and being "probably sufficiently overserved with adult beverages" when she got the call in March 2020 that BioReference was going to launch COVID-19 testing in the Melbourne lab, and that two Roche analyzers were headed her way. That was her last day of vacation for a year and a half. On its first day of COVID-19 testing a few days later, the Melbourne lab ran 3,000 specimens, and by the time the NBA Bubble started taking shape it was servicing many clients, including physicians, hospitals, urgent care facilities, drive-through sites for the general public and the Hospital Corporation of America (HCA), the largest hospital chain in the country.

Eva recalls that she and her staff felt honored to be part of the NBA testing program that was making it possible for the teams to resume playing. "We had many pep talks," she remembers, "Every person, from the courier staff, to the specimen handlers, to the processors, to the lab assistants to the technicians worked together to make it happen." Even a small error in what might seem to be a menial task, like pipetting, could mess everything up and slow the process way down, so thorough training and precise execution was essential. With 10,000 specimens coming in every day from various clients there were times when the lab was struggling to get everything done, and for Eva and her colleagues it was particularly touching and encouraging when visiting BioReference staff from a totally different division, like sales, would take a look around at how hard everyone was working and volunteer to help for a few hours, saying something like, "Can you teach me how to pipette?" Toward the end of the Bubble, although they weren't able to visit, the NBA staff and players in the Bubble made a thank-you video for Eva and her staff to express their deep appreciation for the off-site heroes of the Bubble.

Working with the NBA in the Bubble was demanding in many ways, but for everyone at BioReference it was also highly rewarding because the association has a long-standing and sincere interest in both medicine and healthcare not just for its players, but for the public in general. This dates back to the days of Magic Johnson, and his transparency about his HIV-positive condition, and the work the NBA did with Columbia infectious disease experts. In its preparations for the Bubble the NBA had worked with virologists, epidemiologists, and other infectious disease experts from across the country to make decisions on player safety, how they should practice, how they needed to track the virus, how often they needed to be tested, how quickly the virus spreads from one person to another, when players could come back after having COVID-19, and how people would be allowed in and out of the Bubble. Throughout our time working together, the NBA was genuinely interested in gleaning as much helpful scientific and medical information from their testing processes as possible, and every PCR specimen they had collected in the Bubble included a nasal swab and one swab from the back of the throat, to maximize viral information garnered in the lab. On the advice of their advisers the NBA was our first client that ever insisted we report out cycle times, which was a challenge we met in less than two weeks. And the results of every NBA test were sent to Yale, for further evaluation in terms of genetic sequencing to identify the specific variant of COVID-19 and to rule out any transmission from people living off-site entering the Bubble into the Bubble. The NBA was also very community-minded, and they sponsored mobile COVID-19 testing sites that we ran in the local communities near the Bubble in Orlando and donated new-to-market point-of-care tests to Florida Health in Orange County. Working with such a meticulous, thorough, and scientifically ethical organization was a privilege for all of us, and one the lab would enjoy for three seasons.

Over time the NBA Bubble became a phenomenon in the world at large, inspiring a couple of lively and very popular Twitter accounts that, as described by the *New York Times* on July 20, 2020, "chronicled the world's best basketball players shotgunning beers, dancing with their teammates, failing at fishing and going about everyday activities, like getting haircuts and eating pancakes." The Twitter posts, the *Times* went on to say, "detail the mundanity, and sometimes absurdity, of life in quarantine for the players as they restart their seasons, at Walt Disney World near Orlando, Florida."[4] The BioReference staffers who were working so hard to keep everything moving smoothly in the Bubble may have experienced some of the "absurdity" the newspaper article refers to, but they did not feel anything mundane or everyday about their situation or their activities. Northern Florida had become a COVID-19 hotspot by the time the Bubble began, and for everyone working in the Orlando site and at the Melbourne lab, the stress of working nonstop 24/7 on tight deadlines was ratcheted up to an insane level by the unknown nature of the virus. Eva McCoy recalls that during this period at the lab one cleaning crew after another would quit because they were afraid to handle any of the waste that was associated with COVID-19. As if things weren't chaotic enough already, almost every day Eva would receive calls from the NBA with new and urgent requests.

"We had carts with thousands of specimens waiting to go on the analyzers," Eva remembers, "and I would literally get down on my hands and knees and go through every cart to find the specimen." There was one lab employee named Crystal who seemed to have special powers when it came to choosing a specific cart and reaching into it to miraculously find a specific specimen. "Crystal, get your crystal ball and come over here," Eva would shout out to her when those urgent calls came in. "I'll take over the pipetting. You come do this."

So many laboratory workers across the country worked tirelessly to get as many people as possible tested as quickly as possible during the pandemic, and I believe they sometimes found it disheartening that they received so little public recognition for their heroic work. And their work really was heroic. The nurses and doctors and other healthcare workers

4   Sopan Deb, "Who Is Behind Those N.B.A. 'Bubble Life' Tweets?" *New York Times*, July 20, 2020 (updated July 23, 2020). nytimes.com/2020/07/20/sports /basketball/nba-bubble-life-twitter.html.

on the front lines during the pandemic were highly praised, and rightly so. But very few people ever think about what the testing process itself involves, and therefore the world at large never really focused on what people working in laboratories and other areas of COVID-19 testing were going through. In the case of the NBA Bubble, and later on with other sports testing programs we ran, the public's lack of appreciation for the sacrifices made by our teams who were conducting COVID-19 testing was often compounded by the criticism from the press about the work they were doing. "How come you are giving such priority to super athletes when it comes to testing, instead of to the general public?" This was a question I was asked over and over, and the implicit attitude that came with it was: You guys are assholes. But the truth is BioReference never turned anyone down for testing. We tested everybody who came to the door. At our peak, when we were testing 80,000 people a day, the maximum number of tests for professional athletes within that total would have been about 5,000. Barely 5 percent. When members of the press questioned me or criticized our sports testing programs in terms of the issue of priority and who should be tested, I would remind them that by providing a safe environment where these teams could keep playing we also were helping hundreds and hundreds of working-class folks keep their jobs. Because of our testing and screening programs, these people were able to continue to go to work and support their families during the pandemic. In addition, the NBA Bubble gave the whole country an enjoyable distraction in the midst of the grim pandemic and a sense that normal life might still be possible. In an August 2020 story in the newsletter *TrueHoop*, writer Henry Abbott summarized the remarkable success of the NBA bubble: "A month after the teams boarded planes to a pandemic hotspot, the NBA still has zero confirmed positive cases. That's zero cases not only among twenty-two teams' worth of players, but also among the entire assembled microclimate of 1,400ish staff, media, vendors, league officials, and others. The NBA might be, for now, the United States' signature victory over COVID-19."

On October 11, 2020, the season ended when the Los Angeles Lakers beat the Miami Heat in six games in the NBA Finals. Over the span of 107 days, the NBA had played 172 games in the Bubble at a reported cost of $180 million. They had recouped a reported $1.5 billion in revenue by the end of the season. We had performed over 150,000 COVID-19 tests for them, with a zero-positivity rate among players or team staff within the Bubble. During one of our executive meetings near the end of the season I mentioned to our BioReference NBA team that I wanted to buy a Wilson brand basketball and paint a face on it similar to the face Tom Hanks paints on the ball that washes ashore and becomes his adopted and inanimate friend "Wilson" in the movie *Castaway*. I suggested that we could hang our basketball-person in the executive conference room where we held our NBA internal meetings, as our mascot and "spiritual guide" as we made hundreds of decisions about the NBA testing programs. One day, during a somewhat uninspired meeting, I remarked that several of the executive team members reminded me of Hanks's friend Wilson: they were "dour-faced, full of hot air, and mute when coming up with new ideas." One of the team members chose this moment to inform me, somewhat tersely, that the "Wilson" in the movie was not a basketball. He was a volleyball. I stood corrected, and I had to eat crow for several weeks as emails with pictures of basketballs dressed up as different characters kept arriving in my inbox.

For BioReference, that first season in the NBA Bubble was a steep learning curve that delivered many rewards. The decision to move forward with point-of-care testing was one of the most important decisions the company made relative to how we performed during the pandemic. As a result of our investment and expertise in point-of-care testing for the NBA, we wound up performing millions of rapid tests for multiple different entities around the country, and became the leader in the country for surveillance testing. Other sports leagues and their experts and advisers were watching us as we developed our rapid testing systems for the NBA Bubble, and talking to each other to determine the best practices for the athletes and what was working and what wasn't. Everyone had the same goal: to resume their season as safely as possible, making the health of their players and staff their highest priority.

As it turned out, our experiences in the NBA Bubble would be just the beginning of BioReference's adventures with professional sports leagues. During that first season with the NBA we received word that we had won the contract to do COVID-19 testing for the National Football League. We would be testing all thirty-two NFL teams—players, coaches, support staff, and employees—in their home cities across the country. As we started to study what it would take to set up COVID-19 testing operations at both the training facilities and the stadiums for thirty-two football teams that were headquartered in thirty different US cities, the NBA Bubble, which had involved setting up multiple testing sites within the confines of Disney's ESPN center in Orlando, suddenly began to look like child's play.

Leadership Reflection #5: Pick Talented People and Stay Out of Their Way.

Every leadership book will tell you that the most important issue is the people you pick to be on your team. BioReference had many talented people who were essential to our success during the COVID-19 crisis. None had navigated a pandemic before, none had dealt with most of the industries we partnered with, and few had worked in such a demanding and stressful environment. Point-of-care rapid testing was a huge new challenge for the BioReference teams working in the NBA Bubble. But by working together, they prevailed in a big way. If you pick talented people, give them responsibility, put them in an area where their skill sets are best suited and stay out of their way, they will get the job done. Some executives know how to lead their people, generate intense loyalty, and can get great results by the strength of their personality. Some have tremendous operational skills and know how to drive a process to conclusion. Others have high emotional quotients and interpersonal skills and can navigate through the organization to get things done and some are just really smart and need to be placed in an environment that uses their intellectual firepower. One of the most important attributes of the CEO is to understand who you have around you and how each of their characteristics are best suited to address the crisis. I had the good fortune of having folks with these different skill sets who were successfully deployed to very different responsibilities than their usual position as I reorganized the senior staff to respond to the crisis. They delivered the results that made the program so successful.

CHAPTER 6

4th and Long

As the clock ran out on the 2021 NFL Super Bowl in Tampa Bay, Florida, the BioReference team at Raymond James Stadium jumped for joy and hugged each other. It was not that they were rabid Tampa Bay Buccaneers fans and thrilled that the Buccaneers had beaten the Kansas City Chiefs 31 to 9 in front of 25,000 fans to win the NFL's 55th Super Bowl. The BioReference team was elated because they had pulled off a miracle. On February 7, 2021 the season had come to its normal conclusion, despite all the naysayers who had predicted that COVID-19 would kill the NFL season that year. As the exclusive provider of COVID-19 testing for the NFL, BioReference had performed over 1 million PCR and point-of-care tests for the thirty-two NFL teams in thirty cities around the country so that 256 regular season games, twelve playoff games, and one Super Bowl could be played. Not a single game had been canceled and no player had been pulled off the field because of a false positive result. The NFL's and the NFL Players Association's intense commitment to the safety of its players and staff, and the testing programs and vigorous mitigation strategies put in place to prevent the spread of disease, had resulted in only 329 cases of COVID-19 within the league during the season—a rate of less than .1 percent compared to the national average of 7 percent. We were proud to be part of that historic achievement.

For the BioReference teams that supported our NFL testing program twenty-four hours a day, seven days a week, the 55th Super Bowl marked the conclusion of a tumultuous and often emotional journey that had begun seven months earlier in June 2020 when we first received the news that BioReference Laboratories had won the NFL COVID-19 testing contract. Our understanding was that the NFL steering committee for COVID-19 testing had screened approximately sixty laboratories from around the country—and they had chosen us. Looking back, I believe there were two major differentiating factors that helped us win: first, we were the exclusive provider of COVID-19 testing for the National Basketball Association (NBA) and for Major League Soccer (MLS) in the Orlando Bubble, and thus had experience dealing with major sports figures; second, although the country was only three months into the pandemic at the time, BioReference already had a reputation as the go-to company for designing custom COVID-19 testing programs for a variety of unusual, nontraditional clients.

When I signed the contract and thanked the NFL commissioner Roger Goodell for his confidence in BioReference Laboratories, he assured me we would "hold hands" and work as partners to get through the upcoming challenges. My discussions with the NFL's chief medical officer, Dr. Alan Sills, were equally encouraging. Alan is a brilliant neurosurgeon, and I found it an immense help when he and I engaged in open and calm communication, physician to physician, as we began to address the complicated medical issues that arise with testing for infection during a pandemic.

The enormity of what we were taking on hit us when we met with the NFL players' association and the team trainers to discuss what it would take to execute a comprehensive program for all thirty-two NFL teams—testing their players, coaches, support staff, and employees—in thirty cities scattered around the country. Operating the self-contained NBA Bubble on one large site was nothing compared to the testing system we'd just been asked to develop for the NFL. The stakes for BioReference were no less than gargantuan. The expense for any tests that missed the turnaround requirement would be on us. If a player missed a game because of a wrong result or if a game was canceled as a result of our inability to deliver accurate results in a timely fashion, the financial penalty to BioReference would have been substantial.

Fortunately for us, the NFL executives were willing to expend any and all resources to make sure that they could play football for the entire 2020/2021 season. They were committed to doing everything as safely as possible, and Dr. Sills and the NFL health and safety team had researched the effectiveness of different testing programs in great detail, taking into consideration the number of people who would need to be tested and the frequency of testing. The assumption was that we would use only lab-based PCR testing, which is considered the gold standard in terms of accuracy. In our initial meetings, the NFL proposed to concentrate testing around a small cohort of individuals—those who "touch the ball," so to speak—who would be tested possibly two times a week. But the NFL quickly realized that we would need to expand testing to a much larger population that included all players, trainers, and staff—essentially anyone who might have reason to enter the training facility—and to increase the testing frequency to a daily, if not a twice-daily, schedule. In addition, we would need to develop a solution to test the referees who were traveling to the games from their hometowns around the country.

One unexpected curveball the NFL threw at us early on in these discussions was that to ensure that each training facility remained a safe and secure Bubble in and of itself, they did not want any testing to occur within these facilities. We would need to identify and set up a safe space for people to get tested outside the training facility, and that space would have to meet all the certified CLIA-waived lab regulatory standards for collecting COVID-19 specimens. Only people who had tested negative within a designated time frame would be allowed into the training facilities.

Our chief financial officer, Kevin Feeley, who had set aside his CFO hat to take the lead role for the NFL operations, suggested setting up large FEMA-style trailers as testing sites in the parking lot outside of each team's training facility. It was a great idea, but not simple to execute. Each of these trailers needed three or four examining rooms as well as an office, and each had to be set up so that people could enter at one end, check in, get swabbed, and exit at the other end. In addition, each trailer had to have internet services and computers and any other electronic or IT accessories needed to run our computerized accessioning and tracking systems—and of course, running water and bathrooms. Finally, each testing trailer would have to pass inspection for strict environmental and safety protocols and obtain the necessary permits from both the city and the state in which it was located—and these protocols varied from city to city and from state to state. Kevin, with David Steinfeld (who had substantial experience in the world of professional sports), and Vinnie D'Orazio (who had a long history of running complex lab operations), worked around the clock to get the testing trailers for all the NFL training facilities in place and staffed by midsummer. We assigned a project manager full-time to resolve the permits in conjunction with our legal team who did the research to determine what needed to get done to get us up and running. In two months we had the permits and trailers operational for all thirty-two teams.

* * *

Another unusual request that the NFL made, once again to maximize safety and minimize potential spread of the virus, was that each NFL training facility have a dedicated BioReference team that worked only at that facility—they could not work at any other team's facility or at any other BioReference testing site of any kind. We agreed to this and committed to having ten to twelve full-time employees at every NFL site, including a designated team leader who would be the supervisor for all specimen collection and all site issues.

Speed in turnaround times (TAT) for test results was of utmost importance to the NFL—coaches needed to make roster and training decisions in a timely manner for every practice session and every game— and in our contract we had committed to a quick turnaround time. Originally, we had planned to do the majority of the NFL testing in our New Jersey facility, but to guarantee the fastest possible results for specimens that were being gathered from all across the country we decided to send the NFL specimens to our lab facilities in California, Texas, Florida, and Maryland as well as to New Jersey. We got to work ramping up our COVID-19 testing capabilities in all of these labs—an undertaking that proved particularly challenging in the in the Maryland laboratory, which up until then had been a dedicated genetic testing center with little or no experience in the PCR high-throughput testing needed for COVID specimens. (I am proud to report that the Maryland lab staff quickly committed to bringing up COVID-19 testing, and they became so proficient that at their peak they were able to perform upwards of 20,000 specimens a day.)

To maintain fast turnaround times for all the NFL specimens we developed and implemented a plan to maintain direct control over the specimens by either driving the specimens or flying them commercial air with a designated employee. The logistics plan was complex. We divided the country into five regions based on the location of our five testing labs in New Jersey, Florida, Texas, Maryland, and California. Several of these labs had not performed complex testing like COVID-19 testing so needed a fair amount of work to get them prepared to receive and test COVID-19 samples. Our Maryland laboratory, which up until then had been a dedicated genetic testing center, had little or no experience in the PCR high-throughput testing needed for COVID-19 specimens. (I am proud to report that the Maryland lab staff quickly committed to bringing up COVID-19 testing, and they became so proficient that at their peak they were able to perform upward of 20,000 specimens a day.) We assigned five or six NFL teams to one of these five labs based on time to drive the specimens from the team facility to the lab or flight availability in and out of the team city to the lab home city. In the past, we frequently sent blood samples via FedEx, but FedEx had a minimum delivery window of twenty-four hours and didn't work on weekends, so FedEx was not an option. Some of the NFL training facilities used preseason in Michigan, Montana, Minnesota, Arizona, and Washington State—were far enough away from our COVID-19 testing lab that we would transport the samples by a combination long-haul (driving long distances) using two or more couriers or a combination of land courier and commercial air travel.

Specimens that required airplane transport turned out to be much more challenging. In theory, special couriers we referred to as "flyers" maintained custody of these specimens during transport from the test site to the airport, during the flight and all the way from the destination airport to the lab. Specimens were always packed strictly according to TSA protocol to avoid any contamination, but like all biological specimens, they had to be labeled "BIOHAZARD" in large, easy-to-read letters on the outside of the box. In some of the early runs our flyers made, they simply carried their box of specimens on board with them and stashed them in the overhead compartment. This avoided the issue of checking them as baggage and losing time at baggage claim, not to mention the risk of lost baggage. But this was during a pandemic—not that many people were flying, and those who did fly were jumpy. We don't know if airlines received any specific complaints, but some of the airlines began insisting that according to TSA protocol our flyers needed to check their boxes at the gate when they boarded the plane—in the same way you might check a baby stroller on the gateway before board-ing and then retrieve it just as you exit the plane. We got a letter from the manager of a Delta Airlines department called "Dangerous Goods regarding the transport of UN3373 Biological Substances, Category B," specifically informing us that our packages must be gate checked with a pink tag, and then retrieved at the jet bridge upon arrival. Once the flyers had retrieved their boxes at their final destination, they would drive them to the laboratory. Over two years during which hundreds of thousands of specimens traveled on airplanes, only one box of from one team was lost on a plane. Despite intense searching at the time, the box could not be found. It had simply disappeared into the bowels of the jet. Six weeks later we received a call from the airline: Could we please come retrieve our BIOHAZARD box? We picked it up and tossed it into the trash.

The risk of flight cancellations as a result of inclement weather was always a risk to turn-around-time for those teams that depended on spec-imen transport by air. As part of our mitigation strategy, we set up agree-ments with local hospitals and other regional labs to perform the testing for us in the event that we couldn't get specimens to our labs in a timely fashion. As it turned out, we never had to tap this option, but we had to have it in place just in case.

In addition to developing a logistic program for all of the teams, we were also asked to develop a program to test the eighty referees who were needed to officiate at each game every week. Some of them lived in very out-of-the-way places and traveled long distances each week to get to the game. We used our national at-home testing program to swab them at home several days before the game and separately transported those specimens to the nearest testing facility.

In order to track the location of every single specimen we made the investment into "chain-of-custody tracking," a custom-designed technology that allowed us to track every single specimen at all times, from the moment of collection through transport to the lab through the multistep testing process in the lab until the moment when the final result was delivered back to the NFL. Keeping track of the whereabouts and status of every individual specimen, not to mention all of the ongoing daily operational issues of thirty-two NFL teams, each of which had its own multiple tiers of testing priorities with different testing schedules, was a massive undertaking in terms of managing all the data in real time. We decided early on that we needed to centralize everything and build a "command center," which was a room with multiple screens that displayed a highly complex computerized system that tracked every aspect of the NFL operation twenty-four hours a day. The command center was run by Vinny D'Orazio, who was reporting to Craig Allen, our chief operating officer at the time. Craig is a top-notch operations leader with a long history of successfully running complex lab operations. "We started it and built it as we ran," remembers Vinnie. "It was a massive evolution in a short period of time."

The process flow began every day with a schedule of when the collections were to occur for every individual on each team. Specimens were tracked all day on an hourly basis, using GPS monitoring that showed where every single courier with specimens was at any given time—including any specimens on airplanes—as well as the departure and arrival status of any relevant flights and the expected and actual laboratory arrival times for every specimen. Once specimens were in the laboratory, a system tracked each one through its laboratory process, including which analyzer it was run on and when and how it was reported out. All of these systems were engineered into a single dashboard that could be pulled up remotely on a computer screen. The NFL had their own command center staffed twenty-four hours a day and would track the whereabouts of every single specimen hour by hour from its collection in the field to its result in the lab.

Between the two command centers, we needed to make sure that every person and every specimen was accounted for and on track. Did the driver make it to the lab, did the plane take off on time, did the plane land in the right city? Occasionally, we received some curious GPS data that needed further investigation—in one case we had a driver near Pittsburgh who appeared to have stopped traveling for several hours en route to the lab. It turned out he had a flat tire and was stuck in a ditch. In another case, a Louisiana driver, on several different occasions, appeared to stop for several hours at the same place along the road en route to the Florida lab. It turned out, he was stopping at the same motel each time, for a . . . "nap." Couriers were instructed to always have the specimens in their possession—although there was one instance when a courier had chest pains while driving to the lab and had to call an ambulance. As he was rushed to the hospital by ambulance, this heroic courier clung to his box of specimens, refusing to let go until someone from BioReference arrived to retrieve it. Throughout our partnerships with the NFL and other sports teams Ronald Rayot, another terrific employee who has been with BioReference since 1988 and was working in the logistics department at the time, kept a spreadsheet called "Elite Adversity Challenges" that documented every incident, and exactly how each problem was addressed. In the column headed "Issues," entries included "Transformer Exploded," "Driver Went Missing," and "Hurricane Elsa."

The command center team worked twenty-four hours a day, seven days a week, taking turns as to who would get some sleep. Although they eventually trained other staffers to watch the data for a few hours at a time during slower periods, supposedly so that they could get a break, Kevin, Vinny, and David remember finding it a challenge to stay away from the dashboard. Vinny stayed in constant communication from his home at night, where he often slept on the couch in his living room with his laptop nearby because he knew he would be making and receiving "at least eight calls" every night, and he didn't want to wake up his wife. The creation and operation of the command center turned out to be a game-changing innovation in our partnership not just with the NFL, but with other sports teams and so-called "big employer" clients in the future.

We always maintain the highest standards of patient confidentiality with testing, as required by law, but the NFL had some special issues when it came to confidentiality. Any leaked information could have significant ramifications, not only for the opposing team's strategy in any upcoming games, but also for anyone who might be gambling on the game. Guarding the knowledge that a quarterback had tested positive for COVID-19 twenty-four hours before kickoff (and therefore probably would not play) was a huge responsibility, and the NFL made it clear that we would be held responsible for any break in patient confidentiality or any tampering with specimen integrity. At one point in our discussions, a league executive suggested that we take the players' names off the COVID-19 samples and use code names for them instead. "How do I know your logistics driver will not pull over, take a COVID-19-positive specimen and pour it into our quarterback's test on the ride to the lab, to move the game and bet on it?" he asked. We rejected the idea of code names on medical specimens, but we did agree to add a layer of oversight for NFL specimens by putting a tamper-resistant device on each specimen. In addition, every member of our logistics team signed a non-gambling confidentiality agreement.

Another sensitive issue we encountered in our first weeks of testing for the NFL was potential discrepancies between how quickly various teams received their results. Teams located closer to one of our facilities (the New York Jets and New York Giants, for instance, a mere fifteen minutes' drive to our New Jersey facility) could get their results hours earlier than teams who had to have their specimens flown to our labs. It was perceived as a competitive edge for one team to know who would or would not be able to play and start training earlier than another. Eventually we developed a plan with the NFL to standardize our protocols and release results to the teams that was fair and equitable to all teams. Whether or not we should release news of a positive result was another prickly question. In the end we all agreed that in the interest of patient and community safety, we would inform an individual patient of a positive result immediately, without waiting for the results for the entire team.

I mentioned that Mother Nature was one of our most unpredictable and challenging adversaries when it came to running our NFL testing operations smoothly, and on July 21, 2020, only three weeks after we had signed the NFL contract, she landed a doozy of a blow when Southern California sustained an earthquake of 4.4 on the Richter scale. Vinny remembers getting a call from our Burbank lab with the news, "We had an earthquake, and we lost a couple of Hologic analyzers with NFL batches and we have to shut down and reboot and do reruns. We're not going to make turnaround time. We failed."

The analyzers for COVID-19 testing are highly sensitive to detecting the virus, which is great, but they are very fickle and persnickety in other ways and prone to frequent breakdowns. They were not built to rattle around during an earthquake. As a result of the earthquake, we had to close down our Los Angeles–based COVID-19 testing laboratory to reboot and revalidate all of the testing equipment. This meant that the tests for the five teams being tested at our California facility (the Arizona Cardinals, LA Rams, SF 49ers, Seattle Seahawks, and the LA Chargers) would not make the turnaround time.

Mother Nature walloped us again just ten days after the California earthquake on July 31 when Hurricane Isaias came blowing through southern and central Florida. By this time, we'd become pretty savvy about how to handle bad weather in Florida—Disney had its own meteorology department, and they kept us informed vis-à-vis adverse weather conditions that could potentially affect the Bubble—and in anticipation of the hurricane, we closed down our lab in Melbourne, Florida, and rerouted those five teams' specimens (Miami Dolphins, Tampa Bay Buccaneers, Atlanta Falcons, Tennessee Titans, and Carolina Panthers) to our Maryland lab. Two major disasters in ten days. Okay, we had to scramble a little for each, but we recovered.

Just a few days later, when I walked into our morning COVID-19 testing update on Monday, August 3 (we were meeting twice a day to address a multitude of ongoing testing issues), I was told that there had been an incident the day before. I have always hated delays when it comes to receiving bad news. I prefer to know about any issue as soon as it happens. As a vascular surgeon in my prior life, I told my residents in training to call me anytime, day or night, if there was an issue. I didn't want to walk into the lobby of the hospital and be approached by a family asking why their relative was back in the ICU, or back on the ventilator or had had some major set-back without my knowing about it beforehand. During the pandemic, it was not just my dislike of surprises in general that made me want to hear about any problems as quickly as possible. COVID-19 testing was new and uncharted territory with a myriad of potential challenges and complications, and I wanted to help our team think through any hurdles we encountered to make sure we considered all options. Different divisions in the company sometimes would weigh whether something was important enough to elevate up the chain of command. I told to them to always err on the side of informing me.

"What now?" I asked, feeling slightly annoyed that something had happened over the weekend and I was just now going to hear about it.

"Our driver transporting the COVID-19 specimens for the Tennessee Titans to our Maryland facility hit a deer at 2:00 a.m. in the morning and totaled his car," said David.

"How's the driver?" I asked.

"Oh, he's fine. Couple of cuts and bruises, no real significant injuries. But the car is totaled," said Craig.

"Where are the specimens?" Kevin asked.

"We had a driver go to the scene of the accident and pick up the box of specimens and drive them on to the Maryland facility," said Craig,

"Okay," I said. "How's the deer? "

"Not so good," said Craig. "He's dead!"

"Can we get the head?" I asked. "We could stuff it and mount it in the war room to remind you guys to call me right away when something goes wrong. Or maybe I could put it in my office, I have always wanted one of those deer heads or some big animal mounted on my wall."

"All right," I said, looking around at everyone in the meeting. "So, let me understand this: earthquake, hurricane, dead deer, all in a little over two weeks, right? Anybody want to guess what's next? Maybe locusts?"

Silence.

"Does anybody here actually know about the locusts and the other disastrous nine plagues imposed on Egypt as listed in the Bible?"

Silence.

"Okay. Without Googling the answer, can anyone name any of the ten plagues? Blood—the water of the Nile turns into blood; frogs everywhere; lice throughout the land; flies, millions of them everywhere; pestilence to all of the livestock; boils on everyone's skin; hail from the skies; darkness everywhere all of the time; all of the firstborn children die. By the way, I assume you guys saw the report on National Geographic that the current locust outbreak in Africa and Southeast Asia is the worst in the last seventy years."

"You do know, Dr. Cohen, that you're the only person in the room who would watch National Geographic, is willing to admit to it, and would waste valuable mental real estate by committing the ten plagues to memory?" said Natalie.

"Okay, point well taken." I nodded.

The truth is, if we had known what was going to happen in just two weeks—an event that forced us to shut down the entire NFL program, and brought us close to losing us the NFL contract—I have no doubt that everyone in that Monday-morning meeting would have agreed: We'll take a swarm of locusts anytime!

From the Day of the Locusts to Super Bowl Sunday

BioReference's dreaded Day of the Locusts, so to speak, came on August 22, 2020. Dr. Jim Weisberger remembers being at a restaurant with his wife that evening in downtown Ridgewood, New Jersey when he received a call from CFO Kevin Feeley with some troubling news: a Roche analyzer in the Elmwood Park lab had resulted thirty to forty positive cases in a row. This was highly unusual, and more alarmingly, potentially disastrous for the NFL because these positive results were from players and staff members. Jim immediately left the restaurant and headed to the lab where he found that out of three Roche analyzer runs of 1,000 samples each, there had been eighty-four positive results. Upon further examination, he determined that all of these "positives" fell into a very low-level range of viral presence that was known as "presumptive positive."

"Presumptive positive" was an unpopular term with some of our clients, mainly because a presumptive positive test result could be triggered by exceedingly low levels of virus in a sample—sometimes when there were only viral particles. In many people's minds presumptive positives were actually "false positives," but according to FDA protocol at the time, even when results fell into these very iffy ranges in terms of viral presence, regulations required that they be reported as "presumptive" or "possible" positives. Certain clients in particular hated the term "presumptive positive." Nursing homes, for instance. Almost every day, Jim had to field an angry call from the director of some nursing home who would scream, "What are you trying to do, shut down my facility? Reverse the result!" Sports teams especially didn't like presumptive positives, because they could wreak havoc with their player rosters and game schedules.

When the NFL got the news that as many as eighty-four NFL play-ers and staffers across a platform of twelve different teams had suddenly tested "presumptive positive," they had a fit. The positive results were for people who were being tested every day. They wanted to know what the hell was going on—something had to be wrong.

To understand the nuances here, and to properly lay out the story of what actually happened, we need to wade into the clinical weeds briefly to look at how the so-called COVID-19 "assays," or clinical tests, that are run on various analyzers are designed to work. As a general rule, the high-throughput COVID-19 analyzers detected the virus by looking for the presence of the viral genome within several areas of the specimen. When you look at several areas in a single specimen, it is possible that some areas will test positive and some will test negative. In the case of the Roche analyzer, two areas of the viral genome—referred to as target one and target two—were tested. If you got a positive in either one of those two target areas, no matter how faint a positive and even if the other area tested negative, you had to report the test as presumptive positive. Although Jim and his lab technicians hadn't yet focused on this on that day when the swarm of NFL "presumptive positives" landed in our lab, the potential gray areas between positive and negative results were even fuzzier with COVID-19 assays because all COVID-19 PCR tests had been designed for symptomatic patients. This meant they were designed as highly sensitive tests that could detect the most miniscule amount of virus present in patients. The tests had not been designed for large-scale screening of populations with no symptoms.

In the first twenty-four hours after our presumptive positive "locusts" landed, Jim and his technicians were madly experimenting, swabbing surfaces, running various tests, and analyzing every bit of data to try to figure out what possibly could have caused the burst of what would eventually prove to be false positive results from the Roche analyzers. At the time, they didn't consider the role that the highly sensitive design of the test itself might have played. With our contracts to test various sports teams, BioReference was, at that point, the only lab in the country doing mass screening of a specific group of asymptomatic people on a daily basis. In some sense, our sports league testing programs were a trial study for how the sensitivity of COVID-19 PCR tests could skew results in large groups of people without symptoms. We retested all of the NFL players and staff members who had tested "presumptive positive," and this time every one tested negative.

In the meantime, the press was in a frenzy, predicting that the NFL season would have to be canceled, and the NFL, while under extreme pressure on many fronts, was threatening to cancel our contract. Not having had time to fully explore the implications of the presumptive positive results in this unprecedented situation, Jim came to me and said, "Well, the only possibility I can think of right now is a contaminant in one of the hoods or one of the reagents. I need more time to figure it out, and I need Roche to help me explore some other possibilities." I needed a "Get Out of Jail Free" card from the board game Monopoly, or some magical force that could grant my wish to make this all go away very quickly. I thought of "Zoltar," the animatronic fortune-telling machine in the movie *Big* that grants twelve-year-old Josh his wish to be "big" by turning him into an adult (played by Tom Hanks). I have always been fascinated by Zoltar machines. Friends of mine send me pictures of different Zoltars from around the world whenever they come across one. There is a nice one on the beach near the Santa Monica pier in California. My wish for Zoltar? "Make the errant NFL results disappear."

I considered my more realistic options and made an executive decision: the only way we were going to get through this from a public perspective was to admit that it was our fault—whether or not it was—and move on. In my opinion, you can't fight the press on a bad story, so you take responsibility, apologize, and move on. I spoke with Roger Goodell who was under intense pressure from several owners to cancel the contract and move to another vendor. To his credit, he stuck with us and agreed we would just move on. On August 24 I released a statement:

On August 22, BioReference Laboratories reported an elevated number of positive COVID-19 PCR test results for NFL players and personnel at multiple clubs. The NFL immediately took the necessary actions to ensure the safety of the players and personnel. Our investigation indicated that these were most likely false positive results, caused by an isolated contamination during test preparation in the New Jersey laboratory. Reagents, analyzers, and staff were all ruled out as possible causes and subsequent testing has indicated that the issue has been resolved. All individuals impacted have been confirmed negative and informed.

Although the press continued to rant and to fan the flames of hysteria for another week or so, my strategy worked. We put several new protocols in place to mitigate the NFL's concerns, including an expedited rerun confirmation process for any positive or presumptive positive result and the dedication of certain biology safety hoods in each lab for use on NFL specimens only. The hubbub died down, and we all got back to our respective duties. For Jim, however, the day of the locusts was not yet over. As he continued to crunch the data, examining results from specific analyzers in the New Jersey and Florida labs, he began to connect the dots and see a pattern that suggested that some of the analyzers were too good at picking up tiny amounts of the virus and reporting the results as positive when the patient had no clinical disease. At one point, engineers from Roche actually came to our labs—in the middle of the night, without any notice—and commandeered the Roche machines and tried (unsuccessfully) to prove that the false positives from their machines were the result of contamination in our lab. The FDA got interested in the story and called Jim and asked to set up a Zoom meeting.

"When I had to face the FDA all by myself, and they had literally ten people who were experts in regulation on their team, that was probably the most stressful event of my professional career," remembers Jim who, as someone who worked twelve hours a day seven days a week for two years during the pandemic, is certainly no stranger to stress. Jim presented all his data to the FDA, and they agreed—there was no evidence of contamination. They conceded that most likely a specific lot of reagents, combined with the specific assay, had been overly sensitive when used on asymptomatic individuals.

"I never got a letter saying, 'You are right' from anybody," remembers Jim, "but if you have the facts and the data, they can't argue with it." Publicly, BioReference had taken the hit as having had a local contamination—a nasty word in the world of laboratories; but privately, at least, we had been vindicated.

Fortunately, this crazy hiccup in our NFL testing program occurred during preseason, and on September 12, with all the various players back in place and the plague of presumptive positives in the rearview mirror, the official NFL 2020–2021 season kicked off. All the elaborate systems we had designed to test players and staff daily at their training facilities and deliver results in a timely fashion had to be redesigned to accommodate conditions during the season proper, when there would be two teams at every game location, not to mention the teams' respective owners and their guests (owners each were allowed a maximum of three guests) and referees and various other officials flying in for the games.

Our teams developed and followed very strict protocols for every aspect of the testing of every single person who might be on-site or on the field and coordinated with the command center for minute-by-minute tracking of every single specimen collected. For many of the BioReference staffers who were working for the various teams, the NFL season was an extremely exciting and rewarding experience. Over time, the relationships between our dedicated staff at each training facility testing site and the specific NFL team players and personnel they were testing grew to be remarkably close. The coaches, players, general managers, and even owners of the teams learned their names and became fond of all of the BioReference employees they interacted with on a daily basis, and often mentioned them in their social media posts. As the season rolled forward, the BioReference employees traveled on the team planes to test everyone before away games. They were often included in the team photos taken at these events.

Send in the Fans

Fall 2020 was an insanely busy time for BioReference as an impatient, pent-up, locked-down population began to agitate about how to get out and about. In addition to our sports teams, we were in talks with schools, colleges, universities, cruise lines, airlines, correction facilities, corporations, state and city governments, hospitals, healthcare centers, pharmacies, and every other imaginable vertical about COVID-19 testing programs. As the end of the year approached, and the prospect of the NFL playoffs and the Super Bowl began to loom large, we began to discuss the protocols for bringing fans back into stadiums. Fan testing was a controversial topic at the time, because COVID-19 was spiking across the country as the colder weather came on, and many states were still forbidding large group gatherings of any kind. The Golden State Warriors spent a lot of time and money developing an elaborate plan to get their stadium at Chase Center at half-capacity with regard to fans' attendance by their season opening, but the plan had been rejected by the San Francisco Department of Public Health in November 2020. Fan-less games had been approved, but the feeling was that it was too soon to let the public in—best to stay hunkered down for now.

I was surprised, therefore, when in late December, almost nine months after New York Governor Cuomo had called to ask if we could provide additional COVID-19 testing, I received a call from his senior staff asking if we would consider testing fans for the Buffalo Bills play-off game. New York was one of the states that enforced stringent rules about big gatherings at the time and did not allow groups larger than one hundred people to assemble. But the governor had talked with the owner of the Buffalo Bills, and he was ready to make an exception and allow fans to attend the Bills' upcoming playoff games—with the caveat that for each game every fan would show valid proof of having recently (within forty-eight hours) tested negative for COVID-19 before entering the stadium. Wow. This was a pretty wild proposition—especially since the first playoff game was less than three weeks away. After further talks and negotiations with various representatives from New York State and the Buffalo Bills, we agreed to do it. I thought about who within the organization might have the leadership qualities and experience to tackle the Buffalo Bills' playoff games and decided to call Ryan Kellogg, a senior executive from our sales division and an ex-military guy with terrific take-charge leadership qualities.

"It was Christmas Eve, December 24," Ryan remembered when I asked him about the call. "I had these grand plans for a couple relaxing days leading into the New Year. About 5:00 p.m. my phone rings, and the screen says: 'Dr. Cohen.' I thought maybe you were calling to wish me Merry Christmas."

"Hi Ryan. Merry Christmas, Happy Hanukkah, Happy Kwanza, whatever," is what I actually said when Ryan answered. "I have a new amazing once in a lifetime opportunity for you to spend the next couple of weeks freezing your ass off in the winter wonderland of Buffalo, New York." I explained the project to Ryan, and he immediately accepted.

"All right, great," I said. "Let's set up a call for the morning."

"Dr. Cohen," Ryan said, "tomorrow is Christmas Day."

"All right," I said. "Then set up a call for the next day."

In the next few days, Ryan took a skeleton crew with him to Buffalo and began working out the logistics for how we were going to test a horde of Buffalo Bills fans in one day, moving them in their cars through a massive drive-through testing site we would set up in a parking lot outside the stadium. The Bills had said they wanted to bring in 5,000 fans, but when they saw that we were actually building the testing site, they got excited and upped the number to 7,500. How many lanes of traffic would we need, how long would each test take, what if traffic backed up down the highway? What if it snowed? There were so many questions about how everything would work—not to mention the stunt might need to be executed twice, because there might be two playoff games. As Ryan remembers it, as they attacked all these questions, his team suddenly realized that the biggest elephant in the room was: Who's going to swab the people in the cars, and who's going to transport the specimens back to the lab in New Jersey? They began talking with temp agencies about hiring and training 125 people, basically overnight.

The Sunday before the first playoff game the Bills opened their ticket sales window and were sold out within the hour. When fans bought their tickets, they received a link to a BioReference online system where they could fill in their identifying information and schedule a time for their drive-through on testing day. The night before the first testing day, Ryan and his team, along with twelve members of the Bills staff and eight members of the New York State Department of Public Health, ran a dress rehearsal. The next day, Wednesday, they went live with thirty lanes of drive-through testing. The date was January 6, 2021. By 6:00 a.m. the vehicles were lined up as far as the eye could see, waiting for the chains to drop so that testing could begin. Ryan gathered his crew around him and gave them a quick pep talk: "This is our time. This is what we have prepared for. Be ready. We're going to battle."

"It was almost like a scene from *Field of Dreams*," Ryan remembers. "Build the testing booths, and they will come." And come they did, caravans of cars full of rowdy, excited Buffalo Bills fans, many of them decked out in full Buffalo Bills regalia and chanting "Let's go Buffalo!" Many vehicles held multiple fans that needed testing, including one party van that came through the line with about twenty-five people inside. Everyone was so excited—among other things, it was the first time the Bills had been in the playoffs in twenty years.

The media was there in full force too, and our communications director Hillary Titus was rushing around wrangling various TV vans and camera crews and reporters, scheduling them for quick interviews with Ryan when he could spare a few minutes. It was bitterly cold, and ten 10 x 10 tents had been set up at intervals in the parking lot, with electric heaters inside, so that the testing staff and others could relieve each other from the bitter cold and go warm up. All the swabbers had to be in full PPE, with latex gloves, lab coats, and face shields that kept fogging up and even freezing over with ice. Ryan remembers having to double up on lab coats, with people wearing one coat on their front and one on their back because "our staff was dressed as if they were going snowmobiling, and we only had medium-size lab coats."

At one point, as Ryan was walking across the parking lot, a car pulled up to him and the window rolled down and the woman behind the wheel said, "Hey, Ryan. I just wanted to say that you guys are doing such a great job. We love the support from BioReference. I left some Krispy Kreme donuts for you and your staff." Ryan thanked her, and thought to himself, "What a nice woman." As she drove away the head of operations for the Bills walked over to Ryan and explained: "That was Kim Pegula. The wife of Terry Pegula. They own the Buffalo Bills."

Although the BioReference team on-site in Buffalo had anticipated and prepared for potential chaos and possibly even bad behavior from such an excited and rowdy crowd of sports fans, everyone was well-mannered and compliant throughout the process. "Basically, we brought a bazooka to a knife fight," Ryan remembers, "but that was not a bad thing." For fourteen hours, the fans were pulling up to the test booth in their vehicles and presenting their cell phones. We would scan their phone, and their patient demographics would then be transferred to BioReference's electronic system. Then we would scan the barcode on the tube that their swab specimen was going into and those electronics would correlate with their information in our system as well. Then they would be swabbed. All the specimens were carefully counted—twice—against a master manifest before being packed into coolers that our long-haul couriers would then load into their vans for the six-and-a-half-hour drive to our New Jersey lab. There were three long-haul departure times: noon, 4:00 p.m., and midnight. Amazingly, as the day progressed, everything seemed to be going just as planned.

Our whole testing day operated like "a well-oiled machine," as one local paper described it, but in the end the day was not without some chaos. Hillary remembers running back and forth madly, trying to manage demands from "a full court press," when suddenly all the TV vans and local reporters started packing up and leaving.

"Where are you guys all going?" she asked. "Are you all on the same shift?"

"Hillary, we don't know if you know what's going on in the Capitol," they explained, "but there's significant rioting at the Capitol. We have to go cover that. We'll be back tomorrow." The U.S. Capitol in Washington, D.C., was under siege by an angry mob. It was a terrible day for the country, but one small silver lining for us was that the press did not witness what happened shortly after they left, when one of our tents went up in flames as the heater lit it on fire. Ryan and an off-duty volunteer firefighter in full Bills regalia managed to put the fire out by smothering it with dirt.

At the end of the day, the massive drive-through testing was a triumph. The BioReference team had successfully swabbed 7,500 fans in fourteen hours. But the pre-game process was not over. The BioReference team knew that inevitably there would be ticket holders who did not make it to the testing site that day, or who for some reason would not receive their results, or who would fail to realize that they needed to show a valid negative COVID-19 test to enter the stadium on game day. In anticipation of this, when the long day of drive-through testing was over, the team began to break down the toll-booth operations and to set up a new program for point-of-care (POC) rapid on-site testing. As it turned out, almost everyone received their results within twelve to fourteen hours of being tested, and there were only about fifty-five people who fell through the cracks and needed to take advantage of our on-site POC testing before the game. The positivity rate among the 7,500 fans was very low—less than 2 percent—and almost everyone who had bought a ticket got to attend that January 9 wild card playoff game between the Buffalo Bills and the Indianapolis Colts. The BioReference team watched the game in a conference room in the Buffalo Marriott (also owned by the Pegulas) where they were staying, and Ryan remembers having somewhat ambivalent feelings about which team he was rooting for. After all, if the Bills won, he would be back out in the cold setting up the massive tollbooth drive-through site again to test the fans who bought tickets for the divisional playoff game against the Baltimore Ravens one week later, on January 16.

With 7,500 COVID-19–negative fans watching and screaming in the stands, the Bills did beat the Colts, 27 to 24. Ryan and his team had to set up their testing operation and do it all over again. It snowed on that second testing day, but everything went just as well as on the previous testing day, if not better. The team had learned from their earlier experience, and pulled everything off with fewer lanes of testing and a smaller staff. About half an hour before the divisional playoff, the Bills gave Ryan and his colleagues tickets to the game.

"It was really neat to look around and see that every single person in that stadium had been swabbed by BioReference," Ryan remembers. "A lot of pride was flowing at that point." And as luck would have it, the Buffalo Bills won again, beating the Baltimore Ravens 17 to 3. Unfortunately, the Bills lost to Kansas City the next week in the conference championship, 38 to 24.

Our 2020 to 2021 season partnership with the NFL finally drew to a close with the Super Bowl on February 7, 2021, when the Tampa Bay Buccaneers beat the Kansas City Chiefs 31 to 9 at Raymond James Stadium in Tampa Bay, Florida. Five days later, an ESPN article, "How the NFL navigated COVID-19 this season: 959,860 tests, $100 million and zero cancellations," described what the NFL and BioReference had managed to accomplish together over the previous seven months.[5] In the article, the NFL's Dr. Allen Sills made an important philosophical and medical point about the NFL's decision to test rigorously and to play through their season: part of a physician's job, he explained, is to help people find ways to "coexist with illness or disability while trying to move forward with their lives. That's the nature of medical practice." Another quote from Dr. Sills in the same article was particularly gratifying to all of us at BioReference: "Our NFL facilities and team environments were some of the safest possible locations in those respective communities over the course of the season."

Several months later, at the annual NFL owners' meeting, I was invited to talk about our experience. I reminisced about all that we had been through, including three hurricanes, one earthquake, one dead deer, a fire aboard a commercial airplane carrying specimens that forced an emergency landing, one box of specimens on a commercial flight that was lost in cargo and not found until six weeks later, our at-home testing program for the referees, and a host of other unexpected challenges and surprises.

Many of the surprises were good. Our testing teams bonded with their team players and staff over the months, and a sense of a shared mission kept morale strong during some tough times. A commitment to doing the right thing was another value all the team members shared, and it was evident in every employee at every level of the company. At one point an employee named Mary Joyce, one of our so-called flyers (the couriers who escorted the NFL samples on flights), was featured in several newspapers after she found a stuffed animal some child had left behind in the Detroit Metro Airport. Mary took the abandoned toy—a cow named Austin—with her on her remaining flights, and then posted repeatedly on social media until she managed to get the beloved toy back to his rightful owner, an eleven-month-old baby named Rae from Ohio.

"I have seven kids, and my two sons are both autistic, and they are very, very attached to their plushies," Joyce later said in an interview with the Detroit Free Press. "I know what would happen in my life if either of them lost their stuffed animals, so I picked him up." It was a feel-good

---

5   Kevin Seifert, "How the NFL Navigated Covid-19 This Season," ESPN.com, February 12, 2021. espn.com/espn/print?id=30781978.

story—something everyone needed during the pandemic—but it was also a story about empathy and a commitment to doing the right thing.

In early 2021, on BioReference's fourth-quarter 2020 investors call, I was able to report that the company had performed 1.23 million COVID-19 tests for 5,000 NFL staff, coaches and players every day for seven months. We had used about 15,000 different logistical plans to get the testing done so that 268 games could be played, culminating with the Super Bowl on February 7. The infection rate for the season was less than 1 percent. I was also able to report that we were performing COVID-19 testing for all five of the major US sports leagues, namely football, baseball, basketball, soccer, and hockey, as well as for the Winter X Games in Aspen, US soccer women's and men's Olympic teams, and the NBA G league in Orlando. We had executed a first-of-its-kind fan-testing program for the Buffalo Bills, we had garnered numerous high-profile private and government contracts for COVID-19 testing, and we were one of the largest providers of COVID-19 testing for public schools in the country. I was proud to be able to report all of these accomplishments, but what made me proudest of all was the amazing people at BioReference who had made all these good things possible.

Leadership Reflection #6: Respond to a Crisis with Honesty.

When an adverse event occurs, often the response from those involved becomes more significant and more memorable than the event itself. In corporate situations, staff can face enormous pressure from a company's attorneys and finance folks to keep the response minimal, especially if there are concerns about potential damage to the company's reputation and the negative long-term financial impact from possible lawsuits down the road. I have found that when a situation attracts negative attention, the best reaction is to quickly own up to any mistakes, to be totally transparent about what happened, and to describe how you intend to fix the issue so it doesn't happen again. Taking responsibility and admitting error is what the public wants to hear—not silence, not excuses, not obfuscation or delays in getting out the information. The press will eventually dig their way to the truth in any case, so just make it easier by telling the facts as early as you have the correct information.

CHAPTER 7

School Testing: Reading, Writing, Swabbing, and Arithmetic

I grew up in Queens, New York and I am a product of the New York City public school system. I attribute a significant part of my ongoing appetite for learning and my success in life to my public-school education. Both my wife and daughter also attended public schools, and as a result of all of our experiences I have always been a big supporter of public-school education. I was excited when BioReference began talking with New York Mayor de Blasio's administration in the summer of 2020, strategizing about how to develop a comprehensive testing program for New York City Schools that would allow students to return to their classrooms in the fall of 2020 for in-person education.

My March press conference with Mayor de Blasio at the onset of the pandemic, when BioReference committed to a vigorous testing program for the city, had launched what became a substantial relationship with the mayor's office and senior staff. Working together we had developed programs to test the staff at city hall as well as New York Mass Transit Authority (MTA) employees (the bus, train and subway workers). By the fall of 2020, our BioReference teams had developed highly customized testing solutions for all kinds of nontraditional clients, including multiple sports franchises, large corporate and government employers, nursing homes, correctional facilities and companies in the travel and entertainment industries. But a testing program for New York City's sprawling public school system would present a new and unique set of challenges, not just because of the size of the school system itself, but also because it would involve interacting with and trying to coordinate certain specific subsets of people—children, parents, teachers, principals— all of whom can be highly opinionated.

Throughout that summer the mayor's office had been in intense debates with the board of education, the teachers' union, and public health experts about how to safely bring children back into classrooms, as well as about what an ongoing testing program to screen the students, teachers, and other school staff would look like. These debates were complicated by a number of logistical as well as political issues. The New York City public school system is the largest public school system in the country, with over 1 million students in prekindergarten through twelfth grade attending more than 1,800 schools that are spread across all five boroughs of the city in neighborhoods that are among the most diverse in the country. The teachers' union is one of the most politically influential and powerful unions in the country. Parents understandably have their own strong opinions about what is best for their children, and children themselves can be remarkably obstinate about what they will and will not do. City newspapers at the time followed the many heated discussions between various groups about when and if public schools would reopen, whether there would be sufficient teaching staff, and what the potential health risks might be. Twice the mayor had set a date to reopen city schools, and twice he'd had to cancel.

Eventually, however, the mayor and the board of education and the teachers union agreed upon a plan: they would launch what they called "hybrid learning," in which students would have staggered schedules that alternated between days of remote learning at home and days of on-site learning in school classrooms. (Students also had the option, at the time, of choosing to stick with only remote learning.) As for testing, the city would pay for a COVID-19 surveillance program that would test a certain percentage of students, teachers, and staff in every school on a routine weekly basis. Students would need official parental permission to be tested—but testing would not be required for school attendance. Basically, what the testing component of this plan translated into logistically was that on every single day of the five-day school week an average of 5,000, and sometimes upward of 8,000 designated students who were scattered across some 1,400 different city schools, would need to be tested for COVID-19.

In the early fall of 2020, we finally got word that New York City had chosen BioReference to handle the majority of their ambitious school testing program. This was the good news—the bad news was that the heated debates had drawn things out for so long that we now had about two weeks to get the program up and running. As with so many of our previous COVID-19 testing challenges, the New York City Public School testing program would require designing a complex customized program—in this case one that would efficiently and safely test thousands of schoolchildren and teachers and other school staff every day, Monday through Friday, in hundreds of schools throughout the school year. We needed to quickly design and assemble all the various components—scheduling systems, all the PPE and testing supplies, transportation systems, IT systems, specific on-site layout design for the school testing stations and, last but by no means least, a well-trained staff. The teachers' union had already made it clear that we would have to provide the staff to do all the swabbing, because the school nurses would not be participating in the testing program. As an added last-minute stress point, we learned late in the game that in addition to testing students and teachers during the school week, we needed to test approximately 10,000 teachers as well as other school staff and affiliated personnel en masse in the week just before schools were scheduled to reopen after Labor Day. Like just about everything when it came to dealing with COVID-19, this type of school testing program had never been implemented before; there were no rules, no guidelines, no prior examples or even models for a pathway to success. The logistics and the politics of pulling off this proposal were daunting. When I considered who could handle all these nuances and challenges, I thought of Ellen Beausang.

* * *

Ellen Beausang, SVP of advanced diagnostics at BioReference, says she often thinks back to the evening of March 13, 2020, when I called her at home at about 8:30 p.m. "I always say, that's the call I should have let go to voice mail," she jokes. What Ellen is referring to, of course, is that the reason I was calling her that night was to tell her that I was giving her the "opportunity of a lifetime" to lead several COVID-19 initiatives across several different client types. Ellen was a seasoned diagnostic executive who could easily pivot to take on leadership for different divisions of the company. Originally, I had recruited her to lead our cancer testing division, but she had been working on the COVID-19 front lines for many of our programs ever since that March 13 phone call. In the fall of 2020, I asked Ellen and Michael Johnson, a director of phlebotomy and another great take-charge employee at BioReference, to take on the difficult task of getting our NYC school testing program launched—basically overnight.

"It was like eighteen to nineteen hours a day pretty much seven days a week to make it happen," remembers Mike Johnson as he describes how he and his team developed a plan to put over fifty teams in the field every day to travel around to whatever that particular day's designated schools were (these changed day by day) in order to test the required percentage of students. They had to scramble to rent and equip minivans for the teams to travel in, procure all the necessary medical and electronic supplies, figure out the on-site logistics for testing stations in different schools and design the programs that would identify each child individually, confirm that each child had signed parental permission to be tested, and then report every result back to the parents, the school, the city, and the state within twenty-four hours. They also had to hire and train about 225 people to work in teams of four or five per van, with each team consisting of a driver for the van and four "swabbers."

Remarkably, Ellen and Mike and their teams did in fact pull this off, and the school testing program launched on September 9, 2020. The city would notify us every Friday as to what the next week's schedule would look like, including the specific schools to be visited and the names of the children in each school to be tested. Scheduling was often complicated by the fact that some schools were to be tested Monday, Wednesday, and Friday one week and Tuesday and Thursday the next week, to accommodate asynchronous student attendance schedules. The scheduling software we eventually developed to handle these wrinkles and the third-party software applications we applied would prove critical to our success with the school testing program—and to our success with other nontraditional clients we took on later as well.

Every school testing day began at 5:00 a.m., when a designated route coordinator at our BioReference offices would check in with the people from the City's Department of Health who were determining the schools' testing schedules and so-called "thresholds" (the percentage of students who needed to be tested at each school), and then make any last-minute adjustments to the team itineraries for the day and print out each team's finalized schedule. At about 5:45 a.m. the drivers for the vans (sometimes drivers were trained to do double duty as swabbers as well) would start arriving at our warehouse facilities in New Jersey, where they would pick up the van keys and their route schedules for the day, as well as two company cell phones that were preloaded with the information systems that had registered the details of every individual who was to be tested that day. All the vans had been restocked the night before with large wheeled bins that contained all the necessary supplies to test 500 children that day. The goal was to get all the drivers on the road and headed into the city by 6:15 a.m. to pick up their team at a designated meeting place. The swabbing teams had to report to their designated pick-up site by 7:30 a.m. Frequently, there would be ten or more vans picking up at one location, so people had to make sure that they got into the right van for their assigned itinerary for the day. Once they found their van, the team members had to do a temperature check and then fill out a questionnaire about their health on a website link, in order to receive a special pass code that they would have to show to get into each school that day. (Remember, this was still the first year of COVID-19, and scary numbers of people were still dying of the virus.) Everyone was supposed to be in the vans and ready to go by 7:40 a.m., so that they could get to their first school by 8:30 a.m.

Some schools provided reserved space for our vans, but often when a van arrived at a school there would be issues about finding parking. (Shocking that there could be a parking issue in New York City! You would think that the schools would want to reserve parking for the school testing vans, but somehow that never really happened.) After parking, the testing teams would unload the wheeled bin (which weighed about thirty pounds), roll it to the specified testing area within that particular school, and set up two swabbing stations in the testing area. The team leader would alert the point-of-contact person at the school, who would then begin the process of calling in the students who had been prescheduled for testing. A unique double-scanning technology we developed—its official name is "Schedule O," but the swabbers often called it "scan scan draw," because you scanned twice and then took, or "drew," the specimen—made it a relatively quick process to swab the students and link their specimen to both the preregistered requisition and the barcode for the specimen tube. (This also saved a lot of time when the specimens got to our New Jersey lab, because the samples were all pre-accessioned and could go straight to the analyzers for testing.) When they were finished, the team would pack up, return to the van, and head to the next school on their route. Typically, teams would do two to five schools a day, and sometimes more, depending on their route and how many students were scheduled for testing at each school. In planning the timing for the daily itineraries, we figured each team would swab about thirty-five patients per hour.

When a team had finished all the schools on its itinerary for the day, the van's driver would drop the rest of the team back at the place where he had picked them up that morning, drive the specimens back to the New Jersey lab (stopping en route at a specified gas station to fill up the van's gas tank), and deliver the specimens to the lab, where they would be counted and checked against a manual manifest that had been kept all day before being sent on to the lab technicians who ran the analyzers. Before finally heading home themselves, the drivers would deliver their vans to the warehouse, where another team would work on restocking the bins with all the supplies that would be needed the next day. Workers in the warehouse kept the supply chain moving 24/7, and the specimen testing continued all through the night so that results could be reported promptly the next morning. Any positive results were reported immediately to the parents, to the schools, to the city, and to the New York State Department of Health. We had specifically committed to getting lab results within twenty-four hours for this program, and to notifying everyone about positive results as quickly as possible, so that a potentially contagious student could immediately be pulled from the classroom and isolated, and the school could determine whatever further screening protocols they might deem necessary. We also agreed to notify the parents of any student who tested positive with a personal phone call, so that we could answer any questions or concerns they might have. Typically, if a student tested positive his or her class would be shut down until all the students in that class had been cleared to return to school.

In an effort to manage this enormously complex school testing system as efficiently and smoothly as possible, both the City Department of Health and BioReference developed their respective "war rooms," which they kept staffed twenty-four hours a day to address the ongoing needs of the program. We maintained constant communications between our war room, the city war room, and our many teams—including those doing the actual swabbing in the schools, those doing the testing in the lab, those coordinating the daily routes and schedules, and those working in the warehouse, where we had a dedicated area for NYC School testing supplies. In our BioReference war room we had a team of six people who each provided support for about ten of the vans that were out in the field every day, Monday through Friday. Hundreds of calls came in to this war room team every day, asking for help for a multitude of issues that needed immediate resolution: vans caught in traffic, changes in arrival times, students not showing up, the wrong students showing up, add-ons of teachers and staff that needed to get tested and supply shortages in the field. To deal with this last issue, we equipped a couple of dedicated "helper vans" that were loaded with supplies and roamed the boroughs every day, delivering emergency refills if a team ran unexpectedly short of some supply component.

The metrics of the school testing system sometimes created some unusual pressure points. The City Department of Health had specific percentages, or thresholds, of the student population that they said had to be tested every day, but we could only test students who had their parents' signed consent to be tested. Sometimes the threshold numbers just weren't there—maybe the students who were supposed to be tested wound up being absent, or the principal sent down fewer students than expected, or at the last minute a student (or students) simply refused to be tested. But we were still held accountable to all of these metrics: for instance, if we were supposed to test forty students in a certain school on a particular day but only tested thirty-five, at the end of that day New York City wanted to know exactly why we had fallen under the prescribed threshold. We had to keep copious and meticulous notes on everything. The metrics in the system were further complicated by the fact that the threshold numbers could rise or fall, typically in a range of between 10 percent and 20 percent, depending on how the virus was spiking at the time or the positivity rates within a specific school. And if there happened to be a holiday or a teacher-parent conference day or any other reason why the school was closed, we still had to meet the same threshold numbers within the remaining four days of school that week. We did this by reallocating and increasing the staff over the rest of the week to visit additional schools to meet the necessary metrics.

Despite all these potential speed bumps and hiccups, the system worked remarkably well. When we first began testing in the schools there was understandably some initial trepidation from the kids, some of whom had no idea what it meant to have a swab test versus a needle blood test or an injection that they might encounter at their pediatrician's office. We decided to create what we called a visual aid, a kind of cartoonish depiction of how simple it was to get a swab test, and this seemed to help a lot. Ironically, our teams found that the kids were much easier to deal with than the teachers. "We thought we would have the biggest challenge with the kids being nervous," Mike Johnson remembers. "But actually, the kids were often excited to get swabbed. It was the teachers who were more nervous and reluctant to be tested." Although occasionally a student who had consent would refuse to be tested and every now and then a student who did not have consent would want to be tested—and legally we could not do the latter—as a rule the kids were great sports and incredibly cooperative during the entire process. The sensitivity about testing in general, and the uncertainty at that point about what exactly COVID-19 was, caused some tensions between our staff and the teachers in the schools at times.

Some of the hiccups we encountered were far less intense. For instance, we ran into a unique challenge that we could have never foreseen when it came to testing twins. In our preloaded requisition system, each student that was swabbed was identified by the initial of their first name, their full last name, their date of birth, and their class. Apparently, a lot of parents of twins like to name their twins with the same first letter in their first name—so Tom and Tim, or Sally and Susie. When we tested twins who had the same first initial, same last name, same birthday, it caused a problem. We had to assign each twin a different identifier at the time of swabbing, and make sure they and their parents knew how we would identify one from the other when reporting the result.

When I first heard about our "twin-testing dilemma," I flashed back to the time when my daughter Leslie was young and had identical twin girls as friends. These twins were the same age and in the same grade as Leslie, they lived on the same street where we lived—and they were named Lisa and Lauren. Leslie could tell them apart, but I never could, especially since their mother dressed them identically. Coincidentally, my grandson Jackson and I had recently watched (twice) the movie *The Parent Trap*, a very funny romantic comedy about twin girls who were separated at birth so that each of their divorced parents could raise one of them. The girls discover they are twin sisters by accident at sleepaway camp years later, and when they go home they switch places without telling their respective parent, and then try to get their parents back together. (The version of the movie that Jackson and I watched starred Lindsey Lohan, and was a 1998 remake of the 1961 original starring Hayley Mills. I recommend watching both, instead of one of them twice.)

We ran our testing programs for the New York City public schools all through the 2020–2021 school year, as well as through the 2021–2022 school year. In our second year, we added eight teams that provided testing in thirty-two charter schools in the city. We also initiated some testing programs in the Chicago public schools, but the legal issues and the union problems were much more complicated there, and our programs never grew to be as robust as our programs in New York. Several different models for school testing emerged from 2020 to 2022. At one point a test that used a saliva sample instead of a lower nasal swab sample was introduced to the market by several of the industry manufacturers. Jim Weisberger and his lab team had evaluated saliva testing, and we decided not to accept it as a specimen type at BioReference. We had become very proficient with the swab technology, and testing saliva specimens would require substantial changes to our current lab processes. We did not want to introduce parallel specimen types in the lab which might compromise the ability we had to process upward of 80,000 specimens a day. We knew we would lose some business opportunities, particularly some school districts, by not offering saliva as an option, but we could not convince ourselves that it was worth the disruption. (I also struggled with the vision of elementary school children trying to spit into a tube to give the specimen.) We encountered many forks in the road during the pandemic, where we had to pause and make a tough choice about how to proceed. This was one of them. We made some great choices and some bad choices along the way, but looking back, for our company, we made the right decision not to use saliva. It never had any measurable impact on our ability to compete in the market or to deliver on our commitments to our clients.

Another evolving technology which was particularly applicable to student testing was a procedure called "pooling," a model that combined multiple specimens in a single test, thereby decreasing the cost of testing while making screening groups of people more efficient. A number of specimens—usually between five and fifteen—were collected from a group of students (usually within the same class) and "pooled" into one aggregate specimen for testing. If that aggregate specimen tested negative, then all the students in that group test were negative, and probably all the students in their class were also negative. The cost would be less since only one test would be needed to test five to fifteen students. However, there were some significant limitations and drawbacks to pooling. If a pooled specimen tested positive, then you had to go back and test each student in that pool individually to determine the positive student. This elongated the time it took to determine who was positive, thereby leaving more time for contagious spread. In situations where the incidence of positivity was greater than 3 percent, too many people were positive to make pooling an appropriate and effective option. We used pooling in circumstances where we believed it would be effective, however, and there were many successful pooling test programs throughout the pandemic.

I am very proud of the successes BioReference had with its school testing programs during COVID-19. We tested over 1.5 million NYC students from over 1,000 public schools which serve many diverse communities, communities of color, and underserved communities throughout the boroughs of New York City. We never had any untoward events, and we were always treated with respect. No student ever had an adverse health event—not even a single nosebleed—during the entire experience. Hundreds of people helped make those successes possible, and to give credit by naming specific individuals runs the risk of failing to mention many others who are equally deserving. But I would be remiss if I didn't mention four people who worked on the city side of our programs: Jeff Thamkittikasem, director of the mayor's office of operations; Melanie Hartzog, deputy mayor for health and human services; Emma Wolfe, chief of staff to Mayor de Blasio; and Mitch Katz, CEO of NYC Health + Hospitals. To execute a large-scale initiative like our school testing program, we had to have access to people who had the ability and the influence to operate at the highest levels in order to get the job done. To put it another way, these four people who could cut through the bureaucratic nonsense and make things happen. Each of them played a critical role in the success of the testing programs that allowed NYC kids to return to school during the pandemic.

As I mentioned at the beginning of this chapter, I am a product of the New York City public school system. I attended PS 38 in Rosedale, Queens, New York, and in fifth grade I entered the school science fair with a project that involved dissecting a cow's heart. My mother had procured a huge cow's heart from the butcher (they weigh about five pounds) and I dissected it so you could see all the different valves and chambers. I placed the heart in a big bowl filled with formaldehyde and attached different-colored strings to floating tags that identified and described each part and explained how each part worked. I won first place in the science fair. That event in that school gave a very shy ten-year-old boy the confidence that he could be a doctor one day. Public school made me who I am today. I am proud to have led BioReference through the NYC public school testing program and hope that in some small way I have given back to the system that helped define my career.

Although I will always be extremely proud of the program BioReference mounted to test NYC public school students for COVID-19, one thing continues to bother me. Winning the New York City public schools testing contract had been part of a formal RFP process. Unfortunately, like almost every other aspect of COVID-19 testing, price became a significant determinant—and sometimes a significant detractor—when it came to developing a successful, safe, thorough, and efficient program. We ended up negotiating about testing programs with multiple school systems around the country, and the contracts were frequently awarded based on price. That school systems had to negotiate and navigate through a bidding process to determine the best pricing for the testing they needed to get children back into classrooms in public schools is absurd. The federal government eventually decided to provide vaccinations at no cost to everyone in the country, but in the early stages of the pandemic many public schools had to fend for themselves when it came to figuring out how to pay for the COVID-19 testing they needed to get their students and teachers safely back in schools. If the federal government was willing to pay for vaccines, why were they not willing to pay for testing?

Leadership Reflection #7: Frequently Wrong, but Never in Doubt.

One of the most defining qualities in a leader is the ability to be decisive. Whenever we had to make an important decision, I would listen to everyone's opinions and then make the final call myself. The centerpiece of the surgical personality is the ability to act quickly and decisively under pressure, and as a physician and surgeon in the role of business CEO, I had no difficulty making a tough call and sticking with it. If significant evidence emerged that showed we should change course or reverse a decision, I was always open to it. But in general, you don't want people to think you are unsure about something or that they can easily lobby you for a change in direction. When I decided that BioReference would not do saliva testing, we may have lost some business opportunities, but I am convinced I made the right decision for the company.

CHAPTER 8

"The Love Boat"

Imagine you are twentysomething years old, and you are about a year and half into lockdown during the COVID-19 pandemic. You read an ad posted by a local temporary job agency and you sign up for an interview—and you get the job! Your assignment? You will be leaving the Port of Miami on a luxury cruise ship and sailing from port to port with the ship for a week or more as part of a team that will be testing people onboard—crew and passengers—for COVID-19 every day. The job will be demanding and rigorous and it will require special training—but on your off-hours you will be encouraged to consider yourself an onboard guest, with access to all the recreational options the ship has to offer. What's not to like, right? What could possibly go wrong?

I sketch the above hypothetical to get your full attention and to help you understand what I mean when I say forget about the NBA or the NFL or, forget about nursing homes or prisons, when BioReference signed up for COVID-19 testing on board commercial cruise ships we set sail into a strange new realm where federal regulatory oversight would drive our processes. We knew by then that every industry would have a different set of imperatives dictating the specific COVID-19 testing protocols they needed during the pandemic. The sports leagues based their decisions on their assessment of the most cutting-edge scientific information available at the time and maintained rigorous mandatory testing schedules as well as strict 24/7 guidelines for players and staff in terms of masking and social distancing, both on and off the field. School systems made their COVID-19 protocol decisions based on the ever-changing CDC guidelines, the varying rates of positivity in the world at large and in specific schools, and their own opinion of what would work best for children and teachers. But with the cruise line industry, decisions about COVID-19 protocols rocketed to a new and uniquely complicated set of challenges. This was in large part because, from a pandemic perspective, cruise ships functioned as dangerous "petri dishes"—breeding grounds where the virus could flourish and spread throughout an entire population that was contained for an extended period within a strictly defined space—the ship. As the CDC puts it tersely on its website to this day: "Cruise ships are densely populated congregate settings where respiratory viruses, including SARS-CoV-2 (the virus that causes COVID-19), can spread easily among travelers (passengers and crew) on board."[6]

From the beginning of the pandemic the CDC's regulatory watch over cruise lines was particularly intense, and the entire future of the cruise industry—much more so than with either sports leagues or schools or other verticals—was very much at the mercy of this federal agency. A few outbreaks on ships early in the pandemic had prompted the CDC to issue a "no sail" order for all cruise ships in all waters that the U.S. holds jurisdiction over"[7] on March 14, 2020. As the pandemic dragged on and on, the cruise industry began talks with the CDC about what it would take for cruise ships to begin to sail again. The issues under scrutiny in these discussions the CDC's recommendations and proposed protocols seemed to change on a weekly basis. At BioReference, we had been following all the debates swirling around the cruise industry for months, and we knew that at some point, when and if they were allowed to resume their travel itineraries, the cruise lines would need to design and instigate COVID-19 testing programs. With this in mind, I decided

6   "Cruise Ship Travel During COVID-19," Centers for Disease Control and Prevention, November 3, 2022. cdc.gov/coronavirus/2019-ncov/travelers/cruise -travel-during-covid19.html.

7   Sopan Deb, "Who Is Behind Those N.B.A. 'Bubble Life' Tweets?" *New York Times*, July 20, 2020 (updated July 23, 2020). nytimes.com/2020/07/20/sports /basketball/nba-bubble-life-twitter.html.

to proactively reach out to executives within the industry to better understand what their needs would be when they had permission to sail again.

I like to think I have substantial relationships in the healthcare universe and to some degree in the political universe, but luckily for everyone at BioReference, Phillip Frost, the CEO and Chairman of BioReference's parent company OPKO HEALTH, has much deeper connections to a much wider range of corporate leaders throughout the country and around the globe. During the pandemic, if for some reason Phil didn't personally know someone who we were trying to connect with, it would take him a phone call or two at most to get in touch with that person. Between the two of us, we could usually figure out how to contact anybody we wanted to talk to. But with cruise lines, thanks to Phil, our access was particularly robust. Many of the cruise lines are based in Florida, where OPKO is also based and where Phil, who has lived in the state for over fifty years, has a huge presence. When I mentioned my interest in the cruise industry to Phil, he immediately put me in touch with Richard Fain, CEO of Royal Caribbean, the largest cruise line in the country.

In May 2020 I began talking with the leadership of Royal Caribbean Cruise Lines, the largest of the cruise companies, and our talks continued for months as we considered a variety of testing options to meet the CDC requirements for testing both the employees and passengers. It was clear from the beginning that the top executives at Royal Caribbean were concerned first and foremost about the safety of their guests and employees. They were not going to compromise in any way when it came to designing a vigorous testing program that would give them the best possible chance of successfully maintaining a COVID-19–free environment on their ships. To help them prepare and get ready for the moment when they were given permission to resume sailing, we agreed to develop a COVID-19 testing program that would satisfy both the CDC requirements and their own special needs and concerns. I cannot overstate the number of permutations and combinations of possible testing protocols we discussed as we tried to design a system that would comply with the significant regulatory oversight that the CDC was demanding in order for cruising to begin again, as well as the requirements the cruise lines had about maintaining their own standards of safety, efficiency, and a happy customer experience. These cruise ships are huge, with as many as two thousand crew on board when fully staffed, and as many as five or six thousand guests. Although the CDC had some requirements for testing relative to traveling on airlines on flights form out of the country, these were nothing compared to the strict regulatory oversight they required for traveling on cruise ships. To complicate matters, the testing requirements for cruise line travel applied differently to employees versus the guests, to the vaccinated versus the unvaccinated, and to adults versus children—and all these rules could vary according to the specific health requirements of whichever port or country a ship was visiting. We were looking at a mind-numbing set of variables that would have to be executed on an enormous scale in an exotic venue that we had never worked in before—a giant, multi-level ship packed with people that would be sailing from place to place through all kinds of weather across the wide, open sea.

I mentioned in the last chapter that Ellen Beausang, in addition to her role as head of oncology, had been managing a significant number of our COVID-19 testing clients. I asked Ellen to take on our cruise line initiative and she in turn tapped Tom Grehl—a veteran of the diagnostic industry who she had recently recruited to BioReference to help her lead the oncology testing franchise.

"I never really sat in that oncology seat," remembers Tom, now VP for Business Development for Advanced Diagnostics, as he thinks back to his experience when he joined BioReference in September 2020. "The COVID piece had exploded, and things were hitting us from left and right. All kinds of nontraditional clients—schools, entertainment, travel—you name it, *everybody* was looking for COVID tests." Ellen and Tom began to design complex testing programs for both crew members and passengers that would start weeks before a ship sailed, and then evolve in stages as the crew moved into their quarters, the passengers registered and came on board, the ship set sail from its home port, all the way through the cruise until the trip was over and it was time to disembark. The regulations for every stage were extremely strict. Every crew member had to test negative before they could board the ship, after which they had to stay quarantined on board for fourteen days and undergo regular testing to make sure they stayed negative. Many members of the crew had come from other countries, and they were required to quarantine in a hotel—or in some cases on a dedicated "quarantine" ship—for a period before they could get tested and begin a second fourteen-day quarantine on board the ship. Our staff would be conducting the surveillance testing on all crew members throughout this pre-cruise stage, visiting people in various Miami hotels as well as on various ships. Planning the logistics for all of this testing was a complicated operational challenge—and the passengers haven't even arrived yet! Ellen and Tom remember putting together seventeen or eighteen different versions of long and complicated power points for proposed testing programs during this planning period, in part because the CDC guidelines for cruise lines kept changing week by week for the crew and for the passengers.

"We were building these programs, and then all of a sudden, we'd get a curveball from the CDC," says Ellen. "And of course, Royal Caribbean had their own guidelines that we had to adapt to—oh, and by the way, each ship thought they would be doing things independently and a little differently, according to their own preferences, so there could be big variances from ship to ship." One of the curveballs the CDC threw at the cruise lines early on involved the issue of vaccinated versus unvaccinated passengers. At first the regulatory oversight focused only on different testing protocols for vaccinated versus the unvaccinated guests, with no quotas for the percentage of each group allowed on board. But then the CDC issued a new rule saying that 90 percent of the passengers on board a cruise ship had to be vaccinated, with a max of 10 percent unvaccinated on board. This particular CDC curveball affected would-be travelers more than it affected our testing teams—anyone who was unvaccinated would need to plan in advance to secure one of the limited berths available. But down the line, when ships began to sail again, we would encounter plenty of complications of our own when it came to protocols for testing vaccinated versus unvaccinated, as I will explain shortly.

During these planning stages with the cruise lines, some of our biggest new learning curves came from the complicated legal issues we encountered. I'd like to take a moment here to praise our legal department at BioReference, which under the leadership of Jane Pine Wood, our General Counsel, worked around the clock for two and half years during the pandemic as we were hit by a tsunami of new legal challenges—for government and private contracts, licensure agreements, medical permits, leasing agreements, certificates of waiver, physician's orders, and a myriad other complicated but necessary contractual requirements—as thousands of new clients from all around the country reached out to us for COVID-19 testing. Jane and her team of legal eagles had no legal precedent and no federal guidance to help them sort through the issues they were encountering as a result of COVID-19, and they had to try to shoehorn the legal protocols that arose during a pandemic into an existing regulatory oversight structure that was never set up to address mass testing of hundreds of thousands of people every day. States, counties, and cities all had different regulations and permitting requirements about COVID-19 testing, and these regulations could vary within a jurisdiction according to the specific circumstances where testing was being performed. Many of our new clients had no prior experience with the healthcare industry, and had no understanding of healthcare rules, privacy rules, or reporting rules; most of the attorneys on the client side had not dealt with healthcare issues before. They had no idea of the most basic things, like the need for an official "physician's order" for every test and a physician's review for every result, or that patients have to give permission for an employer to see their results. All test results had to be reported via a secure internet interface, known as an Electronic Medical Record (EMR) system in the healthcare industry, where such systems are ubiquitous. But most of our clients had no experience with or knowledge of EMR systems. Every contract that came in the door had its own nuances, and payment terms always had to be negotiated as most testing was not reimbursed. Some clients made outrageous requests, such as wanting us to destroy the results after they were reported—which obviously we could not do. I honestly do not know how our legal team dealt with all of this and pulled it off, executing approximately 900 different contracts for COVID-19 testing during the years of the pandemic—but then their leader, Jane, has been practicing laboratory law for over thirty years and is a true expert in the field. I promised I would make no snarky comments about lawyers in this book so I will begrudgingly—and admiringly—admit that Jane really knows what she is doing.

Jane's legal expertise proved indispensable in our work with cruise lines. She dove in and started investigating all kinds of tricky laws and regulations that applied to collecting specimens for COVID-19 testing on ships that are docked domestically and abroad, collecting specimens on ships in international waters, performing point-of-care testing in all of these locations and transporting specimens from all these places back to our US-based laboratory locations. She discovered that a number of quirky legal complications can arise when you combine cruise ships and medical testing. For instance, for passengers or crew who were citizens of the EU or Brazil or China, special privacy laws involving consent and authorization forms and protocols for transmitting results and for retaining testing records applied if they were tested in the territorial waters of their home country. When we collected specimens or ran testing at ports of call, we were subject to requirements for testing in those countries. All of these special regulations were in addition to the rules that the CDC, the FDA, and the import/export laws had for transporting biological specimens back to the United States for testing. We only tested in international waters, and most of the testing was on the ship with point-of-care devices. When required, we swabbed employees within forty-eight hours of arriving back to the United States and ran those tests at one of our five COVID-19 testing labs.

I have never been on a cruise or even on a cruise ship myself, and I had no idea of the size of the ships or the number of staff and guests they could accommodate. To say I get seasick is a gross understatement, as I get seasick standing on a dock. However, as I watched all of our cruise line programs being designed, I wanted to see and understand our setup both at the port and on board the ship better. I decided to fly to Miami to tour one of the Royal Caribbean ships docked there, and to view our testing facilities and meet with our employees. When I arrived, I was impressed. The ship, the *Celebrity Edge*, was beautiful and had terrific facilities and upscale, well-appointed staterooms. As I toured the ship's casino, however, a vivid memory of a scene from the movie *Contagion* came to me. In the scene, a character played by Gwyneth Paltrow shakes hands with a chef in a casino in Macau, China, and inadvertently contracts a highly contagious, deadly novel virus that then spreads and causes a worldwide pandemic. As the film's scenes unfold, the plotline traces how a new virus from an infected bat spread to a Chinese meat market and then expanded into a lethal pandemic. I shook my head as I thought about how the movie, released in 2011, presents a remarkably prescient vision of what actually happened nine years later when the COVID-19 virus first appeared in China. I shook off my cinematic musings and finished my tour of the casino, walked through our flow process for testing the ship's crew and guests, met with our employees, and escaped without vomiting.

In November 2020, after months of planning and negotiations, we were finally ready to put some of the complicated cruise line testing programs we had designed into play. We started testing crew members in preparation for cruises that would set sail several months later, running through our entire process on simulation cruises; using our employees and volunteer employees from Royal Caribbean we went through every step of the program to make sure that the procedures and plans we had designed would work. During these simulations we realized that one of our biggest challenges was going to be that Wi-Fi on board was intermittent and that communications with the mainland were spotty or nonexistent at times—and this was when we were still in or near port. This did not bode well, as we depended on Wi-Fi not just for normal communications between staff and clients, but also to report the results from our testing devices. Our employees would have to manually record the results and then when back online with either Wi-Fi or cellular data, send the results back to our central IT systems.

After months of dry runs and recalibrating various aspects of our operations, our program with Royal Caribbean officially kicked off on May 17, 2021, as guests began to arrive in the Port of Miami for the May 24, 2021, embarkation of what would be the first US cruise to set sail with CDC approval since the beginning of the pandemic. By the time the ship's guests began to arrive, the crew members had all been testing negative for weeks as they quarantined on the ship. As I noted earlier, the cruise-line guests fell into two major categories: vaccinated or unvaccinated. When the time came to board the ship every passenger—whether vaccinated or unvaccinated—had to show proof of a negative PCR COVID-19 test within the last forty-eight hours. If you were vaccinated, you could then register (in addition to presenting your ticket and ID, this involved a quick temperature check and health screening), check your luggage, and board the ship. The unvaccinated guests were treated differently. If you were unvaccinated, even though you had proof of a negative test result within forty-eight hours of arriving at the port, you still needed to get another test (and it had to be a PCR test, not an antigen test) done at the terminal before you would be allowed to board.

To accommodate the unvaccinated guests (as well as other people who might need a pre-boarding test), our staff had set up large screening areas with point-of-care rapid PCR testing devices within the terminals. Each screening area had three stations: one for registration, one for swabbing, and a third was a holding area where guests waited to get their results on their phone. Anyone who tested positive would not be allowed to board. We had streamlined the testing process, from registration to resulting, to a time-frame of approximately twenty minutes per passenger: three minutes for registration, one minute to swab, and seventeen minutes to incubate and run the test. The different staffing stations for each test included registration, swabbing, incubation, machine operation, results reporting, and cleaning—all registration and collection stations had to be disinfected after each guest. To ensure maximum flexibility in a variety of different setups, we had trained all the staff (many of whom were temps from local agencies) to handle all the different stages of the process.

Despite all our practice in simulations and other elaborate preparations, a few stress points we hadn't foreseen did crop up during that first live-time boarding process for our first cruise. For instance, we learned that day that during the boarding process for every cruise a palpable sense of urgency would grow greater and greater as the moment for embarkation drew near. "You only have this window of time to leave the port," Ellen remembers, "because there are all these governing rules that the ports themselves have. There were times when we were just trying to get everybody through, because these travelers have paid a lot to take this cruise. The cruise lines have to see a negative result to let the traveler on board, and they also have to leave port by a certain time or they're going to be stuck there for an extra day."

"There were times when we had kids who tested positive and we had to tell the kids and their families that they could not go on the family vacation they had planned. Those were tough conversations," says Ellen, as she remembers other tense and difficult situations that could occur during the boarding process. Sometimes a family had to split up as they boarded, because some of them were vaccinated and some were not. Remember, vaccinations were not available for children under a certain age for a while, so families by default would land in the combination vaccinated and unvaccinated category. Another slightly awkward issue the cruise line had to address at embarkation was how to handle the guests' luggage when they arrived at the port. In pre-COVID-19 times, bags would have been immediately sent off to their designated cabin while the guests registered and boarded. Now the bags had to be tagged and set aside in a place that was easily accessible, in case someone tested positive and had to be sent home. The coronavirus had definitely screwed up the smooth systems the cruise lines had developed over the years that allowed guests to board almost immediately upon arrival—but in this case, in the midst of a once-in-a-century pandemic, it was definitely a "better safe than sorry" inconvenience.

On that inaugural run on May 24, 2021, we successfully got everyone tested and on board, and the first CDC approved cruise in over a year left the Port of Miami and headed out to sea. The pre-boarding scramble was over, but for some of our BioReference staff the "fun" had just begun. As I sketched out for you at the beginning of this chapter, fifteen to twenty temporary employees, most of them in their mid-twenties, would be traveling on board the ship as the official testing vendors for the passengers and crew throughout the cruise. Fifteen to twenty twentysomethings, most of whom have never been on a cruise before, who will stay in their own staterooms (though not the luxury ones with balconies, mind you) and who on their off-shift time will be treated as cruise guests—wait, let's not go there yet. We've just set sail for the first time. For now, I'll just ask that familiar question—What could possibly go wrong?—and then return to the sober subject of COVID-19 testing at sea.

Throughout the voyage our onboard staff would be testing crew members, guests, and themselves according to a precise schedule designed to get everyone on board all the way through the cruise and off the ship COVID-19–free. The cruise line designated the specific areas where onboard testing was to be performed and, as it would turn out, these areas would vary greatly from ship to ship. Sometimes the testing area would be an unused ballroom—although if it was carpeted, we would have to get a floor covering to make it meet CLIA standards—and sometimes a stateroom or a suite of rooms. "What we would ask for, in an ideal world," says Tom, "is that they give us an area where we wouldn't have to break down and set up again, because of revalidation and quality control requirements. Eventually we moved toward the model of dedicated staterooms as our testing headquarters." In addition to stateroom-based testing for the guests, we often set up testing areas for the crew within the employee recreation and sleeping spaces belowdecks. (Our staff has described these special crew quarters as "whole other cities" that most guests on a ship never even know exist, replete with lounges and bars with pool tables, Ping-Pong tables, video game machines, and foosball tables.) The rule was that if anyone—guest or crew—tested positive during the cruise, they had to be quarantined until the ship returned to port and then they would be escorted off separately after all the other guests had departed. Any of our employees who tested positive were escorted off the ship and taken to a hotel where they were isolated and received medical attention.

Although our first cruise with Royal Caribbean went very smoothly, during one of the subsequent cruises we did have a small outbreak on board and three of our employees tested positive. The cruise was on its way to the Bahamas, and we were told that our COVID-19–positive staff would be escorted off the ship and held in quarantine at a hotel on the island. We said "no" to that plan, and instead they were isolated in their staterooms until they returned to the United States. We did not want to have our employees "stuck" in another country where we were unsure of the rules and regulations for quarantine and then have to come up with a plan to get them back to the United States. Getting sick and being quarantined in your stateroom for several days, sometimes in a room in the bowels of the ship, being fed through a crack in the door—I'm sure this was no fun for those employees. (I thought we should give them the option to just walk the plank.) But as a rule, I think our employees had a pretty good time on the cruise ships. They were treated as guests during their off-hours, so they could drink alcohol, attend free entertainment, gamble, and use the pool and other recreational areas as they wished. As I said, most of them were under the age of thirty and had never been in this environment before . . . so, okay, now it's finally time for me to admit that, from an HR perspective, trying to manage fifteen to twenty young employees who are working at sea aboard a luxury cruise ship is not for the faint of heart.

"I thought I'd seen it all during my years in this industry, especially because I've worked on the commercial side with sales representatives at national sales meetings," says Ellen. "Those events were nothing compared to some of the employee issues we had to deal with on the cruise lines."

"Yes, it became a bit of a drama," Tom Grehl agrees. "Kind of like *Jersey Shore* or *Real Housewives*, or *The Love Boat*, or whichever of those shows you like to watch." Without getting into specifics, I will just say that we did have a few "issues" with a few of our employees on board ship, requiring us to let some of them go. Overall, however, the staff did a remarkable job, sometimes under very difficult conditions.

Our testing program and Royal Caribbean's multiple other mitigation strategies were a testament to this cruise line's commitment to providing the safest possible environment for their guests and employees. As our program with them expanded, we tested ships out of ports in Miami, Fort Lauderdale, Cape Canaveral, Bayonne, Seattle, Anchorage, Los Angeles, San Diego, Houston, Galveston, Tampa, Baltimore, and San Juan. At one point we were testing on as many as twenty-four cruise ships at the same time. Of course, it was not all uninterrupted smooth sailing. There were some outbreaks and at some point, the cruise lines decided to have a dedicated "hospital ship" for all COVID-19-positive staff, instead of having them isolated in hotels—which may or may not have been an improvement. But overall, our sojourn on the high seas was a great success.

"One of the most important lessons for me from the cruise line experience was the ability to stand up a testing environment—and I mean essentially a lab, right?—in an area that wasn't built to be a lab," says Tom Grehl. "It was amazing, and it was all about the quality. If you do a basic needs assessment in the beginning, and ask people what they want, then you really can build them what they want in a way that is very structured with very careful quality control. In my opinion, nobody did a better job than we did." While some cruise lines attempted to set up testing programs with other diagnostic companies, several of them ended up coming to us instead because our testing programs were rigorous and maintained the highest standards.

Throughout this time, as the CDC changed their guidance, we continued to modify our proposals to adapt to the new regulations and offer different types of testing programs. At the onset, the CDC had required PCR testing only, but eventually they approved point-of-care antigen testing as being acceptable for certain types of patients. The availability of vaccines for children continually evolved, and the rules kept changing on other fronts as well. On every cruise we had to swab any unvaccinated guests near the end of a cruise and rush their specimens to our labs for PCR testing before they would be allowed to leave the ship. As confidence in our testing protocols and programs grew, the cruise lines began offering longer cruises. On these longer cruises we were asked to test all of the ship's crew during the last days of the voyage, and then rush their specimens to our lab as soon as the ship docked so the crew could leave the ship as quickly as possible. This meant that thousands of specimens had to be kept cold for one or two days until the ship docked, and on several ships the only place to store these 2,000 or more specimens was in the small onboard morgue with refrigerated body cabinets. At one point, when Ellen decided that to better understand our procedures on board ships she should take a cruise herself, she traveled on one of the Royal Caribbean cruises to Anchorage, Alaska. Tom kindly suggested that to really get the full experience she should sleep in the morgue cabinet with the specimens—an idea I fully endorsed.

Leadership Reflection #8: Walk the Walk Before You Talk the Talk.

Armchair leadership doesn't work well in many situations, and during a crisis, it doesn't work at all. Throughout the pandemic, as we developed testing models for a host of new situations—for drive-through sites, schools, professional sports teams, Broadway plays, and other big public events—our teams would run up against unexpected stumbling blocks that demanded unique solutions. For the leaders of those teams—and for me as CEO—sometimes the only way to understand a problem well enough to devise a successful solution was to be on-site with the team, in the middle of the situation, in real-time. You sometimes need to walk the walk, as they say—you need to experience a process in person. For our testing programs with the cruise lines, in order to understand operational issues and come up with viable solutions, our team leaders made it a point to visit—and frequently sail with—the various ships where we were testing. Every ship had a different layout and its own itinerary and therefore required a unique setup. I can get seasick just looking at a ship, but a visit I made to review our operations on the Royal Caribbean Cruise Lines was invaluable to my understanding of our work there. Once you have visited an operation in the field, you can better communicate with the on-site team about future issues, even from a distance. As an added benefit, your colleagues will respect you more for having made the effort to experience their working environment firsthand.

CHAPTER 9

I Need a Test, and I Want It *Now*

As the pandemic dragged on into its second year the mood of the American public began to shift from COVID-19 panic to COVID-19 fatigue. "COVID-19: Hopes for 'Herd Immunity' Fade as Virus Hurtles Toward Becoming Endemic" was the headline of a *New York Times* article in May 2021; the article reported that daily cases of COVID-19 remained at near-record levels around the world, "crushing India with a fearsome second wave and surging in countries from Asia to Latin America." [8] Clearly the virus wasn't going anywhere anytime soon, and here in the United States people were impatient to resume some semblance of their daily routine. They were sick and tired of searching to find somewhere to get a COVID-19 test, and then waiting days to receive their test results. They wanted to visit their friends and family, eat in restaurants, go to the theatre, go to movies, go to sporting events, go shopping, play sports, and travel. Many were tired of working from home and wanted to return to the office. They longed to move on with their lives without having to constantly worry about infecting others. But there were two very basic and very frustrating obstacles to all of their longings: a lack of easy access to COVID-19 testing and a shortage of tests that delivered rapid results.

---

8 "Covid-19: Hopes for 'Herd Immunity' Fade as Virus Hurtles toward Becoming Endemic," *New York Times*, May 9, 2021 (updated November 17, 2021). nytimes.com/live/2021/05/09/world/covid-vaccine-coronavirus-cases.

You would think that to develop and distribute accessible, accurate COVID-19 testing that delivers speedy results would be a relatively simple matter. But throughout the pandemic, getting tested remained a problem for many people. Early on, when the fear about possible spread of the disease was intense, access was difficult because even physicians' offices and hospitals—which are in the business of caring for sick people— didn't want potentially infected individuals coming into their private space. In other words, it wasn't just that there weren't enough swabs— there was nowhere to get swabbed. In an effort to address this problem and improve people's access to lab-based PCR testing, several labs and healthcare companies (including BioReference) had tried to develop a combination home-to-lab test kit that would allow people to self-swab at home and then send their sample to a lab for testing. But developing an easy-to-use home kit with appropriate patient instructions and an efficient and reliable system for sending samples back to a lab proved to be much harder than anyone had expected. One unusual hybrid test that was developed by a company called eMed allowed you to order a test kit and then, when you were ready to test yourself, the company would watch you perform the test via live video and verify the results. This model was especially popular with people returning to the United States from overseas, because it was accepted by both the CDC and U.S. Customs as a valid test for reentry to the country. Although several other companies eventually developed other hybrid test kits, at BioReference we were never able to get FDA approval for our home-to-lab kit. We had attempted to develop the home kit in-house but could not get the packaging and patient process simple enough for approval. We could have hired an outside company to develop it for us, but I made the decision that we were too late to the home market and abandoned the project.

Mobile healthcare services that sent a trained technician to your home to collect a test specimen and take it back to the lab emerged as another innovative alternative for COVID-19 testing during this period. In January 2021, under the leadership of SVP of digital health and chief digital officer Richard Schwabacher, BioReference had launched Scarlet Health, a fully integrated digital platform with home visit services that that gave people the convenience of having blood or urine samples taken at home instead of having to travel to a patient service center. We added swabbing for COVID-19 specimens to the home visit services Scarlet offered, and this became a popular way for people to avoid waiting in a long line at a testing site.

While all of these innovations and options for testing helped to some extent, as people began agitating to get back out in the world and pursue normal activities, what they really needed was either an at-home rapid test for COVID-19, similar to the at-home pregnancy tests women sometimes take, or an easily accessible rapid testing site somewhere near them. In August 2020 the FDA had issued an emergency use authorization (EUA) for Abbott's BinaxNow COVID-19 test kit, an at-home rapid antigen test that delivered results in fifteen minutes. "Now, more Americans who may have COVID-19 will be able to take immediate action, based on their results, to protect themselves and those around them," announced Jeff Shuren, MD, JD, director of the FDA's Center for Devices and Radiological Health. But when these at-home COVID-19 diagnostic kits first came on the market very few people could buy them, because the government had bought almost all of them to distribute to the states, which would then decide how to use them. Unfortunately, since they still required a physician's order and were not yet approved for screening patients without symptoms, and the result could not easily be transmitted for data collection, many states elected to put them in storage for several months.

As I described in chapter 4, BioReference entered a steep learning curve when the NBA requested that we set up point-of-care (POC) COVID-19 testing devices in the NBA Bubble in addition to the lab-based testing we were performing. Many manufacturers had rushed to get these devices to market, but no regulatory environment existed for the use of the devices, all of which operated differently. Some POC devices required a trained operator on-site to perform the test, while others were so user-friendly patients could test themselves. Some were PCR-based, while others were antigen-based. There are very important difference between these types of devices. PCR point-of-care devices use similar technology that is used for the majority of testing performed in the laboratories and is highly accurate. If a patient tests negative with a PCR test, it is very reliable in determining that the patient does not have COVID-19. Conversely, if the patient tests positive, regardless of whether the patient does or does not have symptoms, that patient has COVID-19. Antigen-based point-of-care devices look for easily detectable proteins that attach to the surface of the virus, but are less accurate then PCR tests. These tests are extremely reliable if a person tests positive. However, these tests are relatively unreliable if the patient tests negative. In other words, if a patient has symptoms and tests negative with an antigen test, it is unreliable as an indicator of not having COVID-19, which is why many people are told to test several times over sequential days if they have symptoms. In addition, if we are setting up a large screening program to make sure people don't have COVID-19 before they attend an event or go on a cruise, antigen tests are not reliable enough. This is why, originally, the FDA did not approve antigen tests for screening purposes. A physician's order was required for every POC test, and results had to be sent back to the patient, to the state, to the physician of record, and to the Department of Health. When these devices first came to market, most of these devices had no internet connectivity, and results had to be recorded and entered into a database manually.

BioReference had done extensive testing of the POC devices and found that the Thermo Fisher Scientific Accula SARS-CoV-2 point-of-care device was the best device for us to use with our multiple different use cases. The Accula used PCR technology and provided a result on-site in about thirty minutes. In addition, we could connect it to our information systems to report the result and then transmit that result back to the ordering physician, contracting entity, and state as required. It was reliable and worked well in the field, and we could train our folks on how to use it within a short period of time. We ended up using these devices everywhere: large events, small events, screening programs, retail sites, etc., and at one point we purchased the entire inventory of Accula devices that Thermo Fisher had on hand. Like some of our other partner companies, the folks at Thermo Fisher were incredibly helpful, cooperative, and driven to help us do whatever we could to help the country get back to normal. Offering on-site POC testing to the general public as the world began to reopen would be a big pivot for the company. We were already seeing a significant decrease in specimens being sent to our lab from our sites swabbing the general public. General public testing was clearly moving to a more convenient point-of-care rapid solution where a person can get a result within thirty minutes close to where they were. If we were going to stay relevant as a leader in COVID-19 testing for the country, we clearly needed to lean in on providing point-of-care solutions. In addition, COVID-19 testing revenues would help sustain the company until routine lab testing, blood and urine, returned to pre-pandemic levels. When Natalie Cummins and I discussed the situation and debated whether we should hire someone to work exclusively on this new application of POC testing, one of our big concerns was whether we would have enough work to keep someone busy full-time. We needn't have worried. Establishing these new POC testing programs turned out to be as challenging as a full-blown business start-up in many ways. We had recently hired Greg Bokar, who had been working at a medical start-up in Manhattan, and when we put Greg on the team for the new POC programs he hit the ground running and never looked back. Within a month we couldn't figure out how we ever had accomplished anything without him. When Greg first joined the company in November 2020, he had worked with Natalie, Mohit, and Tom to develop the testing programs for the cruise lines we planned to launch in the spring. In January 2021, Greg had gone to Buffalo to help Ryan Kellogg and his team with the Buffalo Bills playoff games. Greg remembers noticing a new dynamic between our BioReference staff and the crowds of people we were testing in Buffalo.

"The Buffalo Bills games demonstrated that fans could start going to events as long as testing was part of the process," says Greg. "But when we were testing fans in Buffalo, we were no longer interacting with people who were employees of a business company or players on a sports team, and therefore getting paid to be on-site. We were dealing with a different demographic that had different levels of expectation and frustration, and we began to feel the added management pressures of a customer service operation." As we ramped up our POC testing programs on multiple fronts—including large-scale screening programs for people attending big events at the Chase Center in San Francisco, at Madison Square Garden in New York and at Barclays Center in Brooklyn—our POC testing teams all felt the shift in crowd dynamics and management pressures that Greg describes. Testing thousands of eager fans or audience members in a brief time span before a special event meant we had to set up a temporary testing site that met CLIA-waived environmental standards, and that had several hundred POC testing stations equipped with the Accula devices, test kits, furniture, medical supplies, printers, computers, cell phones, and Wi-Fi capabilities that would be needed to efficiently run POC COVID-19 tests. It also meant we had to hire and train several hundred people to staff the temporary site. People attending an event did not have to register in advance, but instead could provide their information when they showed up to get tested. Everyone who showed up to attend the event—the exact numbers were often unknown—would need to get tested, wait thirty minutes for their result, and then get cleared to enter the area where the event would take place. The challenges of our POC testing in the NBA Bubble—where testing times for players and staff were scheduled in advance, every patient's information was preloaded, and the volume of testing was both predictable and easily managed—suddenly seemed straightforward when compared to those of mass testing crowds of an indeterminate size for a precisely scheduled one-off event. And of course, once the testing was over and the event was underway, the temporary testing site would need to be quickly dismantled and removed. Nothing like this had ever been done before. We decided to hire another company to provide the physician's order for tests and to follow up with any patients who tested positive. The physician service was several hundred doctors available online to order the test, review the results, and talk with the patient at almost any time. Once again, we developed our own IT systems to report results for each client, and we hired hundreds of new people and trained them how to register patients, how to swab patients, how to run the Acculas, and how to enter each patient's results into a database. We developed strict standard operating procedures about every stage of the process, from registering to swabbing to cleaning between each specimen collection, to make sure we maintained the same high standards in every venue where we tested. I cannot overstate what a gargantuan task it was to pull off this scale of testing in dozens of different venues around the country. Early in the pandemic, when COVID-19 testing had abruptly switched from testing blood samples to testing nasal specimens, our vice president of phlebotomy services, Sue Aveta, had put together the programs to train our phlebotomy staff, who were used to drawing blood, how to swab. Now, as we entered the new frontier of mass testing with POC devices, Sue took command of the army of workers we sent out to run the POC testing sites in the field. Sue did an amazing job managing the thousands of new employees.

"I started at BioReference the week the states began to shut down for COVID-19, my first day was March 23, 2020," remembers Sue, who had twenty-five years of experience in the laboratory industry prior to coming to BioReference. She estimates that by the time she turned her attention to the new POC testing contracts that came in as the world reopened, we had as many as 500 teams working in the field in forty-eight states. Sue and many others on the POC teams remember wild situations as they rushed around to set up POC testing programs all around the country, including times when they had to improvise at the last minute due to supply shortages, staffing shortages, bad weather, device malfunctions, legal issues, power outages and other unforeseen roadblocks. Often, someone from the leadership team would have to fly out from wherever they were based to help handle things. "It was during COVID, so there were always flights available," remembers Andrea Correa, who worked with Sue as a regional Director of Phlebotomy. "It was getting up and going on a moment's notice that sometimes was tough." They all agree that it took every department of the company to orchestrate all of these new testing contracts successfully. "Everybody in every department had one mission, and it was to just get the job done," says Andrea. "I don't know that I worked with anybody that was not a willing participant, that didn't understand what the mission was."

Sports stadiums and other entertainment venues were some of the first companies that wanted to reopen in the second year of the pandemic, but soon businesses of all kinds began to ask us about testing programs that would allow them to bring their workers back to the office. In May 2021 Crain Communications sponsored a videoconference for the New York business community where Eric Gertler, president and CEO of the New York State Economic Development Corporation (the state's leading economic development agency) and I cohosted a discussion on how to get employees back to work. In June 2021, I hosted two conference calls, one for the senior executives of the top one hundred companies in New York and another for the senior executives of the top one hundred companies in Florida, to discuss testing options that would allow large companies to bring their employees back to work. Everyone wanted to know how they could accomplish this safely. Of course, the answer to that question differed, depending on the particular company and its needs. Companies whose employees were for the most part public-facing (grocery stores, transportation systems, casinos, etc.) required different solutions than companies whose employees worked in a private office space. Companies with public-facing employees needed more frequent testing solutions as they were constantly exposed to hundreds of people every day that could be carrying the virus. Companies with office workers only tested their employees when they showed up in the office. Hospitals and health systems needed a different solution, frequently multiple different types of testing, to be able to test their patients, test their employees, and test people showing up at their emergency rooms. Cindy Jacke, SVP of strategic ventures, managed all of our hospital and health system clients. Cindy was another veteran of the industry with tremendous insight into how to service the health system clients.

Over the next months, BioReference designed custom testing programs for many of these companies, taking into account variables such as frequency of testing for different categories of employees, locations for any on-site testing and what to do if an employee tested positive. Many companies had designated a senior executive to oversee their testing program, but frequently we found that this point person had been overloaded with misinformation and confusing guidelines from the CDC, and needed to be "educated" on the realities of a testing program that would make sense for their particular needs. The programs we recommended often involved a combination of lab-based PCR testing and POC testing on-site—but every situation was different and required a unique solution. To further complicate matters, the government regulations about who should get tested and when they should get tested (which varied from state to state) kept changing. For example, some states limited gatherings to a certain number of people and required testing within forty-eight hours of an event. Some states allowed gatherings only if everyone was tested by an on-site device within several hours of an event. For our teams who designed these custom programs, every client was like a giant jigsaw puzzle for which the shapes of the puzzle pieces were constantly changing.

As a result of the streamlined one-stop solution we could offer with our POC rapid testing—we could schedule, swab, test, and get results for people on-site in thirty minutes—BioReference began receiving requests to screen guests for private events such as weddings and birthdays. Weddings could be particularly problematic—suppose someone shows up in black tie or an evening gown and then tests positive? We'd have to say sorry, you look great but you can't go in. For on-site screening at these kinds of events, we needed a dedicated place where people could wait for thirty minutes until their test result was available, without the risk of spreading the infection to others should someone test positive. Sometimes wedding planners who wanted guests to have a lab-based PCR test within forty-eight hours of the first wedding event would ask if we could set up a private drive-through specimen collection site for their guests two days before the event (which we declined to do). Unexpected issues often popped up—for instance, what about the people who were traveling to the event from out of state? Would we accept another lab's results? For one huge bar mitzvah with 250 guests, we tested everyone forty-eight hours before they arrived and then had to do a rapid POC test for every guest on the day of the event before they were allowed to attend. On another occasion a rabbi asked us to test everyone on-site before they were allowed in the room to attend a bris. I am sure the baby boy, not really looking forward to his circumcision, was rooting for someone to test positive, so the event would be canceled! "The combinations and permutations for what people wanted at these private events were infinite and frequently unrealistic," remembers Tom Grehl. But whenever we could, we tried to meet the clients' needs.

As more and more people began to step out of lockdown and into the world again, the market responded to the increasing demand for convenient, quick testing. Several existing as well as new companies began offering rapid testing on the streets of cities around the country, in tents or trailers, and many concierge physicians offered a valuable service by testing people in their homes. I don't mind people trying to make some money by offering a solution in a difficult situation like inadequate access to COVID-19 testing, but it disgusts me when price gouging occurs. We never charged more than Medicare's standard rate of $100 for a PCR test with a small additional charge for our physician oversight service plus the cost for the staff who performed the test on-site. But some of the pop-up testing sites in the city were charging several hundred dollars for a rapid test, and in one outrageous example of price gouging, a friend of mine in Florida was told that it would cost $1,000 per test for him and his family members to get tested in order to take a flight home. Health insurance companies would only reimburse for lab-based testing, and many people could not afford the full price of a rapid test. As so often happens, lower-income people suffered when it came to COVID-19 testing.

Our point-of-care testing expanded into another new and intriguing direction when, in August 2021, we began discussions with the leadership of New York State about how to speed up the safe reopening of activities all around the state in general, and in New York City specifically. At the time, you had to show proof of a negative test within several hours before you could attend most events or eat at a restaurant. As part of a state program that would be called "New York Forward," we agreed to offer "retail" testing to the general public at an affordable price at multiple sites across the State and in New York City. As opposed to the large drive-through testing sites or the programs we set up with specific clients (sports, employers, etc.), retail testing would be like other shopping experiences. The public would walk into a store, purchase a test, get it performed and have a result in thirty minutes. In our effort to open many sites across a wide area in multiple neighborhoods, our plan was to open both within CVS stores and in storefronts that were currently vacant. None of us at BioReference had ever been in the retail business, and just thinking about all of the issues that would come with opening up one storefront, and then multiplying that by twenty or thirty storefronts scattered around the city and state kept me up at night. I decided it was time to call Mitchell Lewis, an old friend of mine who had spent his entire career in the retail industry, and ask him to come on board as a part-time consultant to develop and oversee our retail testing operation. Mitchell had owned and managed several retail clothing operations, including a high-end chain of women's stores. He knew everything about storefronts, leasing, signage, foot traffic, customer service for walk-in clients, and every other retail detail. He also had tremendous digital and online retail experience and knew how to develop a store website, which would be invaluable in handling online communications about our retail POC testing.

As Mitchell remembers it, "Jon called and said, 'There's something going on. I'm not sure whether it's for you or not. What's your bandwidth?' I said, 'I have twenty hours a week.' And Jon said, 'Oh good, that'll work.' By the way, twenty hours a week ended up not working at all." With Mitchell's help, we launched our retail operations through a partnership with CVS drugstores, who generously offered the state access to some of their stores as testing sites for free. "We put small outposts in CVS stores using about 150 square feet in any available corner—a back corner of a stock room, or any space that they could find," remembers Mitchell. "We opened in nine stores with plans to go to thirty—but we never went to thirty, we stopped at nine as the demand was not enough to justify opening additional locations."

As had been the case throughout the pandemic, access—that is, physical locations where we could conduct our testing—once again became our biggest stumbling block. Temporary tents or other outdoor structures would not work because of problems with electricity, Wi-Fi, and varying weather conditions, and we could not afford to rent storefronts unless we made the test very expensive, which we did not want to do. But happily for us, in a brilliant move, the State contacted the Real Estate Board of New York (REBNY) and asked if they could help identify empty street-level stores where we could set up testing facilities for free. The real estate companies were eager to do anything to get people back to New York City and to have businesses begin to reopen. Many landlords had spaces they couldn't use themselves, and several were extremely cooperative and agreed to let us use the space rent-free.

"The landlords were amazing," remembers Mitchell. "They helped us with space, with build-out, with some free utilities. It was a good thing to do. It didn't really cost them anything. They were giving us the locations for free and it was a nice thing to do. But nonetheless, as a retailer, the leases had to be negotiated. It was funny to negotiate a zero-rent lease, funny for us and funny for them. But the leases all needed to be negotiated—I got to know Jane Pine Wood and her BioReference legal team very well."

Awkward moments could arise during these negotiations. "We had an interesting problem because we had to dispose of swabs," says Mitchell. "It's called medical waste, or sharps, at a doctor's office after an injection. Now, we weren't giving out any injections, but we had to treat the swabs as medical waste. We had a company that came into each location every day to remove them, but that was tricky. I mean, in the middle of a pandemic when you're negotiating a lease, you certainly don't want to say to the person you're negotiating with, 'By the way, where is the medical waste truck going to be picking up?'"

All in all, the partnership with REBNY was a huge success—if not financially for us, at least in terms of getting people tested. REBNY is one of those unrecognized groups that stepped in to be very helpful in getting New York back on its feet. In addition to our sites scattered around the state, BioReference had some iconic rent-free city locations for the New York Forward program—including 599 Lexington Ave, Grand Central, 3 Times Square, 4 Times Square, the Oculus (the beautiful new transportation and retail hub near the World Trade Center in New York City, where we tested several dignitaries in preparation for the 9/11 ceremonies in 2021) and 1800 Broadway (across the street from the Ed Sullivan Theater, where we tested for several Broadway shows and for the Tony Awards).

I had asked Richard Schwabacher, our chief digital officer whom I mentioned earlier as the leader of our Scarlet Health concierge home diagnostic service, to create a digital system for our new retail operations with the New York Forward program. I have known Richard for seventeen years, and he is someone who can figure out a way to get anything done. I have watched him take on extraordinarily difficult challenges, navigate the obstacles, and deliver a solution. With Richard taking on the digital systems for retail operations, I now had every senior executive in the company overseeing some part of the COVID-19 business. Richard developed a website where people could go online, enter their basic information, find the testing site closest to their location, schedule their appointment, and pay in advance depending on the type of testing they wanted. Although we only offered scheduled appointments, people often showed up for testing without an appointment or made their appointment when they first got in line outside the facility. We always tried to be accommodating, and to keep sites open if people were waiting to get tested.

During COVID-19 BioReference functioned as a dominant revenue source for our holding company OPKO Health (which is publicly traded), and financial considerations always had to be part of be any contract we offered for testing options. Our POC testing retail operations required a huge temporary workforce and created massive changes in our staffing and supply chain requirements day by day, which called for unprecedented and intense levels of financial analysis within the company. Many times, we had no reliable data and had to make "educated guesses" about whether or not to take the financial risk and go forward with a particular proposal. I was incredibly fortunate to have Adam Logal, the chief financial officer at OPKO and the most knowledgeable finance expert that I have met during my fourteen years in the diagnostic industry, as a partner during the entire pandemic. Adam understands the diagnostic business inside and out and functioned as an "operating" CFO to help manage the company. Steve Rubin, an attorney and OPKO's executive vice president, was another critical player who served as the "voice of reason," as we made some difficult decisions about some of our contract and partner relationships. Steve would analyze the advantages and disadvantages of a particular issue, and always brought clarity to our discussions.

* * *

By the end of the summer of 2021, POC testing and at-home self-testing kits dominated the market. Most people had access to free at-home tests and rapid-testing sites had popped up everywhere. The early-pandemic shortage of testing had morphed into an oversupply of testing options, and we began to scale down our retail COVID-19 testing capacities on all fronts. We had wanted to keep the infrastructure we had built "warm" so that we could turn it back on quickly in the event of another outbreak, and we had asked the federal COVID-19 response team for help with this—but we never received a response from them. In the fall of 2021 we were in the process of taking down our COVID-19 testing infrastructure at all five of our labs when the Delta variant hit, and a second wave of infections raced across the country. Unsure of the reliability of the at-home tests and POC rapid tests, people once again began to clamor for lab-based PCR testing, and we had to scurry like mad to rehire people and bring our testing capacity back to our 80,000 per day range. Within two months Delta had waned, and once again we began to downsize both our workforce and our COVID-19 infrastructure— only to have Omicron explode in December. We found ourselves in the same predicament as when Delta had hit, but this time the situation was worse. We had thousands of tests coming in overnight, and we couldn't rehire people fast enough to perform the volume of testing coming in the door. At first, we were unable to achieve reasonable turnaround times, but we started offering substantial incentives for every shift our employees would agree to work, and we cleared the backlog in four days.

* * *

As I think back to the roller-coaster ride BioReference was on throughout the pandemic, from the abrupt and brutal arrival of COVID-19 to the stuttering ambushes by variant viruses as the pandemic waned, I am reminded of one of the most interesting and insightful movies I have ever seen, a film called *Sliding Doors* (released in 1998, and, yes, another Gwyneth Paltrow movie). The plotline traces the two paths Paltrow's character's life could have taken, depending on one seemingly minor "fork in the road" event: whether or not she catches a train (either she gets on the train and the sliding doors close behind her, or she doesn't get on the train and the sliding doors close in front of her). As the two story lines emerge, whether or not she gets to board the train will define her life as one that achieves success and happiness or one that does not. I believe we all encounter these seemingly minor but actually significant forks in our lives, and I can identify several occasions in my own life where the "road taken" has yielded a very different outcome than the "road not taken" would have. Our decision to push forward with rapid POC testing proved to be a singularly important "fork in the road" event for BioReference. With our decision and subsequent actions, we differentiated ourselves from our two larger competitors as well as from the rest of the market. Our POC programs took us in all kinds of new and different directions, including massive gatherings for one-off entertainment and sports spectacles, businesses of all kinds, private gatherings and celebrations, concierge home testing services, and retail storefronts. Our investment and expertise in providing comprehensive testing solutions with POC testing allowed BioReference to perform millions of rapid tests for multiple different entities all around the country, and we became the leader when it came to surveillance testing.

"Would I do it again?" Mitchell recently considered this question as he thought back to his experiences organizing retail COVID-19 testing for a job that was supposed to be part-time—but definitely was not. "Absolutely. I absolutely would do it again." Testing for COVID-19 in 2021 had its rough moments for all of us at BioReference, but I think we all would agree with Mitchell. We might do a few things a little differently next time, but we would absolutely do it again.

Leadership Reflection: #9: The Enemy of Courage Is Fear.

Every decision to take a risk is, by definition, backloaded with a fear of failure if things don't work out. This fear can make it seem safer to be timid—"nothing ventured, nothing lost." Our executives at BioReference worked as a courageous team when it came to risk-taking; we were ready to accept the decisions we made once we had made them, and to charge ahead to make things happen. We decided to go full throttle on POC testing, which was a huge risk, and we took another risk when we launched retail testing. In the end our POC testing proved profitable, but the retail operation did not. There was no Monday-morning quarterbacking, no snarky, "I told you so." We made our decisions, we owned them, and we tested millions of people for COVID-19 along the way.

CHAPTER 10

Moving Forward:
Fixes for the Future

I suppose the reality that the worst of the pandemic was behind us hit me when Jim Weisberger and Craig Allen (our chief operating officer) asked me if it might be time to mothball the heart of our COVID-19 testing facility in our primary New Jersey laboratory. This central COVID-19 testing area, which we had built during the pandemic, could perform over 35,000 PCR COVID-19 tests a day and now it was sitting idle. I met Jim in the lab, and, as we walked through the facility, I remembered the days when it had bustled with activity as several hundred plastic bins holding thousands of COVID-19 samples were teed up for processing on the analyzers. We had people working in three shifts to keep the operation running twenty-four hours a day. Over the last two years I had visited the facility multiple times a week to deliver a test sample that needed an expedited result for some reason. I would track down the supervisor and make sure the specimen was put on the next run. On several occasions during the pandemic, when access to testing was scarce, I had people stop by my home so that I could swab them (I was fully protected with gown, mask, and gloves) in my garage or through an open car window in my driveway. People sometimes stopped by BioReference to have me swab them in my office or in the lab, and eventually I had a POC rapid test device in my office so that employees could stop by and get tested. Now, it was time to move on and turn our attention back to our core business of running our menu of over 3,000 tests.

As I look back at BioReference's experiences during the pandemic, I can point to several important strategies we embraced that differentiated us in the market and contributed to our overall success during the ongoing crisis of COVID-19. First, we found creative and aggressive ways to apply technologies that already existed to the new challenges we faced. We did this within the scientific domain of our clinical labs, where we worked to validate new platforms and testing procedures, as well as with the digital platforms we developed for field services we provided outside our labs, where we integrated bar-code scanning, tracking software and other advanced scheduling and communication systems to streamline the stages of the testing process.

Second, we hit the ground running and quickly scaled up from a lab-based diagnostic company where all of our testing was performed at one of our five locations around the country, to a nationwide network that offered diagnostic services on-site, in the field, at hundreds of locations around the country. We expanded our staff from 4,000 to 8,000 employees in order to deliver comprehensive turnkey solutions in unprecedented situations.

Third, we learned to interact with every client with open and sensitive ears, paying attention to their specific concerns so that we could adapt our procedures and create the customized solution that would best meet their needs. In addition to these strategies, we had a staff of dedicated people who all had a strong work ethic and who all left their egos at the door as they charged into the battle against COVID-19. Working in the most stressful and often very uncertain conditions, they remained calm, determined, competitive, agile, tenacious, and adaptable. They always found a way not only to get things done, but to get them done in the best way possible. I was incredibly fortunate to have them at my side during this unexpected and unprecedented adventure.

Over the course of this book, as I have described how events unfolded for the diagnostic industry during the pandemic, I have alluded to several of my favorite movies. One of my top three favorite movies of all time, and one that comes to mind now, was the 1985 release *Back to the Future*. I have always been fascinated by time travel and by the notion that one small change in the past could have a massive ripple effect on how things play out over the course of history. In my opinion, *Back to the Future*, starring Michael J. Fox, illustrates this concept better than any other sci-fi time travel movie I have seen. As the film's plot unfolds, a teenage boy (played by Fox) travels backward thirty years in a time travel machine (a modified DeLorean automobile) and ends up almost canceling his future existence by inadvertently interfering with his parents' courtship. In the beginning of this book I referred to the milestone-moment experiences that hit every generation, those bigger-than-life events that people around the world experience simultaneously and later use as reference points in their individual and collective lives. Two examples of such moments for me would be President Kennedy's assassination in 1963 and the 9/11 attacks on the World Trade Center and the Pentagon in 2001. If we had access to a time travel device like the "flux capacitor" in *Back to the Future*, could we go back and prevent Kennedy's assassination, or stop the 9/11 attack? How would history have been forever changed if those events had never occurred? And what if we could we go back to that Chinese meat market or Wuhan lab where COVID-19 first appeared and close the market or lab? Could we prevent the pandemic that has killed almost seven million people? Barring that possibility, we have a responsibility to do whatever we can to be prepared for the next pandemic.

In the wake of the pandemic, a number of people who played high-profile roles during the crisis have written about their experiences, commenting on the areas where they feel the Unites States failed in its response to the coronavirus and recommending changes they believe must be made if we want to prevent similar devastation in the future when the next pandemic hits—which they all agree is just a matter of when, not if. Many of the recommendations these experts make are important, and they concur on many points. For instance, everyone seems to agree on these basic initiatives: we need to reexamine and restructure our overall public health infrastructure in the United States; to ramp up domestic production of all medical supplies; to create government stockpiles of all these supplies; and to establish a clear line of authority in the event of a public health emergency. I believe most people would agree that we also need a more comprehensive program for the surveillance of infectious diseases globally. This latest pandemic increased our awareness of the critical ways outbreaks of disease can intersect with issues of national security, and many experts now advocate the creation of new branches of our intelligence services that could gather accurate and timely information about any new pathogens that may be emerging around the world. Our trust that other countries will share information about new pathogens that appear in their communities in a timely and fully transparent fashion took a big hit during the pandemic, and early detection is critical to the prevention of widespread infection, especially with respiratory RNA viruses like SARS-CoV-2. The sad fact that Black, Hispanic, and Indigenous communities in the United States suffered at disproportionately high levels of disease during the pandemic and struggled with access to testing shines a harsh light on chronic inequities within the US health system.

Unfortunately, as the postmortem discussions continue on how we need to do things differently in the future, I have yet to see a detailed strategy for comprehensive testing in the event of another pandemic. The capability to test large numbers of patients for the presence of an active virus, or bacteria, or fungus, within a reasonable amount of time continues to be a critical issue for the country. As an article in the *New York Times* noted grimly on October 1, 2022:

> If it wasn't clear enough during the COVID-19 pandemic, it has become obvious during the monkeypox outbreak: The United States, among the richest, most advanced nations in the world, remains wholly unprepared to combat new pathogens. . . . New infectious threats are certainly on the way, mostly because of the twin rises in global travel and vaccine hesitancy and the growing proximity of people and animals. From 2012 to 2022 for example, Africa saw a 63 percent increase in outbreaks of pathogens that jump to people from animals compared with the period from 2001 to 2011.
>
> "In people's minds, perhaps, is the idea that this COVID thing was such a freak of nature, was a once-in-a-century crisis, and we're good for the next 99 years," said Jennifer Nuzzo, director of the Pandemic Center at Brown University School

of Public Health. "This is the new normal," she added. "It's like the levees are built for the one-in-a-100-years crisis, but then the floods keep happening every three years."[9]

Although many experts agree that the emergence of a new infectious pathogen that poses a grave risk to global health is inevitable, no one knows what category of pathogen that will be. One of our biggest problems in responding to COVID-19 was that our official pandemic response protocols, such as they were, had been posited on the assumption that we would be able to contain the spread of the virus with vigorous contact tracing and quarantines. No one considered the possibility that we would be unable to contain the virus and would have to test millions of people a day to help control the spread of the virus. To prevent any re-occurrence of the recent pandemic disaster, my key recommendation would be that the country establish and maintain a "ready to test" national lab infrastructure that can perform high-volume diagnostic testing on short notice after an outbreak. The next virus (or bacteria or fungus) that attacks us will almost certainly have a different genetic code than COVID-19 that will require a new "recipe" for detection and new reagents for running a high volume of tests on (hopefully existing) high-throughput platforms. The next virus could require a different type of test sample than the nasal swab used for COVID-19 tests—possibly a skin scraping (as used in testing for monkey pox), a blood sample, a urine or saliva sample. We just don't know. PCR technology will probably remain the gold standard in terms of accuracy, but we will need to develop new point-of-care devices and new at-home test kits. On the upside, because of our COVID-19 experiences the time needed to develop these new recipes and tests should be shorter, and the necessary testing platforms could already exist (although they might be in storage).

The lack of infrastructure and communication between US diagnostic companies—currently a hodge-podge of public health laboratories,

---

9 Apoorva Mandavilli, "New Infectious Threats Are Coming. The U.S. Probably Won't Contain Them," *New York Times*, September 29, 2022 (updated September 30, 2022). nytimes.com/2022/09/29/health/pandemic-preparedness-covid-monkey pox.html.

hospital laboratories, academic laboratories, research laboratories, and commercial laboratories—contributed to the slow ramp-up of testing capabilities and to the failure to develop a comprehensive and coordinated testing plan during COVID-19. But in my opinion, the existing laboratories—regardless of their level of inter-coordination—could never have addressed the demands of COVID-19 adequately and will not be able to provide proficient testing in the next pandemic. The public health laboratories, research laboratories, hospital laboratories, and university laboratories do not have the capacity to perform high-throughput testing for hundreds of thousands of patients a day. The commercial laboratories can process hundreds of thousands of specimens a day, and they have the infrastructure, logistical networks, and IT systems to support high-throughput testing—and they did perform the majority of COVID-19 testing during the pandemic. But I believe that a focused "factory" approach to processing millions of tests a day at several large-scale facilities specifically designed for high-throughput molecular diagnostics would be both more efficient and less costly and would help mitigate the multitude of issues the country faced during the pandemic. Current technology supports testing at these high-throughput levels, and as technology evolves the numbers could increase. If five such facilities could be built around the country, within a short period of time the country would have the capacity to run about five million tests a day. The facilities should be located near international airports across the country, because screening of international travelers may be important in the future, and delivery of supplies and specimens to the lab would be easier and more efficient—the latter would help with quick turnaround times.

The federal government could issue an RFP to build and staff these facilities and create a new Office of Pandemic Diagnostic Services (OPDS) within the federal government (either at HHS or at the CDC) that would have both significant oversight over the new facilities and an appointed leader who reports to the senior leadership structure of HHS or CDC. We should not be waiting until there is an outbreak to appoint a "testing czar." We need currency and continuity to monitor the situation on a day-by-day basis and to stay prepared for potential infectious threats. We should have a well-organized and well-run OPDS that is responsible for oversight of national testing facilities that are on stand-by to test five million people a day within a short period of time after an outbreak. The leader of the OPDS should have regulatory authority over all aspects of testing that supersedes any local and state regulations—a multiplicity of the latter confused and hampered the nation's response to the recent COVID-19 pandemic. Officials at the OPDS also should have the responsibility and regulatory authority to direct supply chains to make sure that the national "factory" testing facilities and all other laboratories get the equipment, reagents, and other supplies they need, and should base decisions about priority on geographic and other factors that will best serve the American public.

Employed together, the new testing facilities and oversight structure would help remove many of the obstacles that prevented adequate testing during COVID-19 in the following ways:

- Supply chain coordination would be much more efficient. If necessary, the president, in conjunction with leadership at the OPDS, could use the Defense Production Act to prioritize the distribution of supplies appropriately. This would guarantee that the greatest number of tests were made available as soon as possible.
- With the bulk of testing data coming from fewer and much larger scale testing sites, meeting reporting requirements to state and federal agencies would be much easier. One of the greatest failures during the pandemic was the lack of reporting capabilities from hundreds of labs across the country. Without this real-time data, it was nearly impossible to provide testing resources to the areas that needed it the most.
- Maintaining quality oversight of testing procedures would be much easier if there were fewer facilities to oversee.
- Keeping sufficient stockpiles of reagents and other supplies in anticipation of another epidemic would be more efficient and easier to coordinate with fewer testing facilities.
- Standardization of state-of-the-art diagnostic technology as new advances continue to evolve would be easier to maintain at fewer facilities. As we experienced at BioReference, technology during a pandemic constantly evolves. Upgrading to the newest

technologies should include rapid point-of-care devices as well as high-throughput platforms.

- The new national lab facilities could become special centers for studying and developing testing strategies for possible pandemics in the future. No such comprehensive facilities currently exist.

Each of the new national facilities would require approximately 100,000 square feet, ideally within self-contained buildings on a single floor with adequate electrical and plumbing services and parking to accommodate several thousand employees. The number of employees needed at any given time would be proportional to the volume of testing being performed. If the facility was operating at 100 percent capacity, on a 24/7/365 schedule with four shifts per week, it would require about 3,000 employees. When in a standby mode, each facility would require a basic staff of about one hundred employees. Based upon development plans for comparable facilities and taking into consideration expenditures for space build-out, the purchase and installation of lab equipment and other necessary fixtures, and licensure and certification fees, it would cost approximately $100 million to build each of these five facilities, with an ongoing cost of $10 million each per year to keep the facilities in standby mode. The cost to stockpile reagents and other supplies would depend on how many days the facility could test for when fully stocked. Ideally the facilities would be able to deliver sixty days of maximum capacity testing when fully stocked, as this would give supply manufacturers some time to ramp up production levels. A total expenditure of about $500 million to build five large-scale testing facilities across the country would be a modest investment compared to the amount that was spent on vaccine development and distribution during COVID-19.

The American public should never again have to scurry around trying to find a drive-through site or some other location where they can get tested if a pandemic occurs, and we must never return to a situation where people have to wait in line for hours to get tested. Every state as well as every county should be required to submit a plan to the OPDS that identifies the specific locations where mass specimen collection can occur in their area. The federal government should develop a plan to send personnel from FEMA, the Public Health Corps, and the National

Guard to conduct the testing at these pre-designated testing sites, and not depend on local municipalities to find and hire staff to do the testing.

Leadership Reflection #10: Communicate Often.

Every good leader must learn to communicate effectively internally to the employees and externally to the public. Effective communication usually includes stories and anecdotes that are relative to the message. I would like to close with one of my favorite urban myths. For me, it is a story about hope.

"Good luck, Mr. Gorsky."

On July 20, 1969, Neil Armstrong put his left foot on the surface of the moon and famously said, "That's one small step for man, one giant leap for mankind." What most people don't know is that after his historic walk on the moon, and as he reentered the lunar landing ship, Armstrong then said: "Good luck, Mr. Gorsky!"

When scientists who were monitoring the lunar landing at NASA headquarters and reporters who were watching heard Armstrong's cryptic remark, they were baffled. They had no idea what he was referring to. When the famous astronaut returned to earth the press asked him about Mr. Gorsky, and he refused to answer. The press scoured his background for a clue, but they could find nothing about a "Mr. Gorsky." At every press conference for the next twenty-three years, whenever he was asked this same question—"Who is Mr. Gorsky?"—Armstrong refused to answer. But after a speech he gave in Tampa, Florida, in 1992, when the press once again asked him about his curious remark, Armstrong paused and said he would answer. Mr. Gorsky had recently passed away, and he felt he could discuss the matter.

When he was eleven years old and growing up in Ohio, Armstrong explained, he was playing baseball with a friend in his backyard one day and his friend hit the ball over the fence into the yard of his next-door-neighbor—a Mr. Gorsky. When Armstrong went next door to retrieve the ball, he overheard Mr. Gorsky in the midst of a very loud argument with his girlfriend, on the topic of whether or not she would marry him. The girlfriend was being quite obstinate, it seems, and as she started to scream at Mr. Gorsky she happened to look out the open window, where she saw Armstrong picking up his ball. "You want to marry me?" she shouted. "Well," she continued as she lifted her arm and pointed at Armstrong, "I will marry you when that kid walks on the moon!"

Good luck, Mr. Gorsky.

For me this is a story of eternal hope because it illustrates that anything can happen regardless of the odds. Mr. Gorsky's girlfriend could have turned to him and said, "I'll marry you when the United States is prepared to test five million people a day in the event of a pandemic." The plans I have laid out in *Swab* are both possible and affordable and would help protect the American public from experiencing tragic and unnecessary deaths, as well as many other traumas, when and if another pandemic outbreak occurs. I just hope that we don't have to wait for the next person to walk on the moon before we get to work to make this happen.

Acknowledgments

I am grateful for the incredible support of Leslie Marshall, who patiently worked with me through countless editorial changes and whose creative wisdom helped me work through the story that is told. She patiently sat through countless hours of interviews with the BioReference employees to fully understand the story we wanted to tell. She encouraged me to think through the leadership aspects and suggested I apply my "fun" knowledge of movies to incorporate into the story. I could not have written this book without her assistance.

My life would not be what it is without my awesome wife, Karen Kostroff, MD, my "I can do anything" daughter, Leslie Cohen, MD, my incredibly smart son-in-law, Brendan Finnerty, MD, and my enchanting two grandchildren, Jackson Finnerty and Colette Finnerty. I am grateful to have in my life my brother, Michael, my sister, Terry, and my niece, Patrice.

I am incredibly fortunate to have close friends who everyday put up with my "craziness," my dark humor, my deep sarcasm, and constant drumbeat of making fun of them in any way possible. I have known most of them for over twenty-five years and have had the privilege of sharing my life's journey with them: Andy and Jeri Casden, Paul and Karen Chaplin, Tom and Joan Facelle, Jeff and Ellen Kraut, Lyle and Karen Leipziger, Stuart and Harriet Levine, Mitchell and Jayne Lewis, Mark and Patty Manoff, Jeff Menkes and Susan Fox, Yaron and Michele Rosenthal, Steve and Cheryl Rush, Roger and Hildy Savell, Henry and Jackie Shaub, Rocco Andriola and Susan Vari, and Alan and Susan Wurtzel.

Finally, this book would not exist if not for the thousands of dedicated employees of BioReference who delivered COVID-19 testing to the nation during the most stressful and often uncertain times as they remained calm, determined, competitive, agile, tenacious, and adaptable. I am also grateful to have had the leadership of OPKO at my side during this journey; Phil Frost, MD, Jane Hsiao, PhD, Adam Logal, and Steve Rubin.

About the Author

Jon R. Cohen, MD was one year into his tenure as CEO and executive chairman of BioReference Laboratories—one of the largest medical diagnostic labs in the United States, serving all fifty states, with over $700 million in annual revenue—when the COVID-19 pandemic struck. Dr. Cohen led BioReference to national prominence during the ensuing health crisis as he and his executive leaders reallocated resources and created teams that spread out across the country and worked around the clock for the next two years, delivering over twenty-five million COVID-19 tests and pushing the company into the limelight as the nation's leader for large-scale screening programs.

Dr. Cohen has more than thirty years of healthcare experience as a seasoned strategic leader and healthcare policy expert with a successful track record of growing new healthcare business ventures. Prior to his tenure at BioReference, Dr. Cohen held high-profile positions that spanned the worlds of medicine, healthcare administration, and politics. Trained as a vascular surgeon, by the age of forty-four he was chief medical officer at Northwell Health, the largest healthcare system in New York State. After serving as a healthcare adviser to presidential candidate Senator John Kerry in 2004, Dr. Cohen ran for lieutenant governor of New York on a single-issue platform: healthcare. Dr. Cohen subsequently joined the administration of Governor David Paterson as the senior adviser responsible for all public policy and strategy. He served for nearly a decade as one of five senior executives at Quest Diagnostics before joining BioReference in the fall of 2019. In November 2022, Dr. Cohen accepted a position as CEO of Talkspace, one of the largest virtual behavioral healthcare companies, serving over one million users. He has previously been named as one of the nation's topmost powerful physician executives by *Modern Healthcare* and is recognized for his popular TEDMED Talk, "Why Don't Patients Act Like Consumers?" In 2020, Crain's New York Business recognized Dr. Cohen with a Notable in Health Care award. A gifted public speaker, Dr. Cohen has addressed many public and private gatherings and has given innumerable TV, radio, and print interviews. He has published two books on vascular surgery, as well as over 100 peer-reviewed articles and book chapters.

A practicing vascular surgeon for twenty years, Dr. Cohen completed his residency in surgery at New York Presbyterian Hospital/Weill Cornell Medical Center and his vascular surgery fellowship at the Brigham and Women's Hospital at Harvard Medical School. He lives in Great Neck, New York, with his wife, Karen Kostroff, MD, chief of breast surgery for the Northwell Health System. Their daughter, Leslie, is a reconstructive plastic surgeon with an expertise in microvascular surgery, and Leslie's husband, Brendan, is an endocrine/head and neck surgeon. Leslie and Brendan have two young children. All four adult surgeons in the family agree that when the time comes, they will not put any pressure on the younger generation about their career choices: both of Dr. Cohen's grandchildren will be free to become any type of surgeon that they please.

Index

Abbott Binax Now, 119
Accula, 58, 120, 122
ACLA, 5–7
Allen, Craig, 50, 73, 77, 133
Antigen testing, xi, 111, 115, 119–120
Armstrong, Neil, 141–142
Aveta, Sue, 122–123
Azar, Alex, 6

Back to the Future, 134–135
Beausang, Ellen, 50, 93–94, 106–107,
    111, 114–115
Big, 80
Bioreference Laboratories, xiii, 28, 68
Birx, Deborah, 5–6
Bokar, Greg, 121
BSL, 4–5
Buffalo Bills, xiv, 83–85, 87, 89, 121
Cahill, Greg, 50
Castaway, 64
CDC, xiv, 3–7, 9, 12, 26, 29–32, 34,
    56, 104–107, 109–110, 112, 115, 118,
    124, 138
Chain of custody, 73
Cohen, Leslie, 25, 99
Commercial lab industry, 5–6, 27–31,
    138

Contagion, 109
Copan diangnostics, 43
Correa, Andrea, 123
Cruise lines, xiv, 83, 104–112, 114–116,
    121
Cuban, Mark, 53
Cummins, Natalie, 13, 20–21, 50,
    54–55, 58, 78, 121
Cuomo, Andrew, 12–14, 17, 24, 83

D'orazio, Vinnie, 70, 73
de Blasio, Bill, 17–19, 21, 24, 91, 101
Delta variant, 36–37, 129–130
Difiori, John, 55
Disney/ESPN sports center, 54–56, 65
DNC, 39–40
Dowling, Michael, 13–14, 24
Drive through, 11–24

Earthquake, 75–77
E-Med, 118
Evans, David, 50

Fain, Richard, 105
False positives, 67, 78–79, 81
Feeley, Kevin, 50, 69, 74, 77, 78
FEMA, 16, 22, 23, 69, 140

Finnerty, Brendan, 25
Finnerty, Jackson, 25, 99
Frost, Phil, 51, 105

Gambling and the NFL, 75
Gertler, Eric, 123
Godfather, 14
Goodell, Roger, 68, 80
Grehl, Tom, 106, 114, 125
Grogan, Joe, 6

Haas, Bill, 22
Hartzog, Melanie, 101
Home kits, 17, 118
Hurricane Isaias, 76

Jacke, Cindy, 50, 124
Johnson, Michael, 94
Joyce, Mary, 88

Katz, Mitchell, 18, 101
Kellogg, Ryan, 83–87, 121
Khani, Julie, 6
Kopy, Mike, 13
Kostroff, Karen, 11–12, 16–17, 25

Labcorp, 8, 22, 28, 30
Lewis, Mitchell, 126–128, 131
Logal, Adam, 129

Mango, Paul, 5, 24
Mathur, Mohit, 58, 121
McCoy, Eva, 60–62
Mohapatra, Surya, 28
Monk, Geoff, 50, 51
Moye, Rachel, 58–60
Mr. Gorsky, 141–142
Murphy, Phil, 21, 23

NBA, xiii, 53–65, 68, 103, 119
NBA Bubble, 55, 58–65, 68, 119, 122
New Rochelle drive through, 8,
    12–13, 15–17
New York Forward, 126, 128
NFL, xiii, 55, 67–71, 73–76, 78–83,
    87–89
NYC Health and Hospitals
    Corporation, 17–18, 101
NYC schools, xiii, 91–94, 97, 99, 101

Omicron variant, 36, 130

Paltrow, Gwyneth, 109, 130
Parent Trap, 99
PCR, xi, 3, 33–34, 41, 48, 56, 58, 59,
    61, 115, 69–71, 79–80, 118–120,
    124–126, 130, 137
Pence, Mike, 2, 5, 20, 23
Point of care, xii, 56–58, 61, 64–65,
    67, 87, 109, 111, 115, 119–127,
    129–131, 133, 137, 140
Pooling, 100
Presumptive positive, 78–82
Priority testing, 45–47
Puritan, 43–44

Quest Diagnostics, 5, 8, 22, 28

Rayot, Ronald, 74
REBNY (real estate board of New
    York), 127–128
Redfield, Robert, 6, 25–26
Retail testing, 126, 129, 131
Roche, 32, 34, 35, 54, 60, 78–81
Rossi, Rob, 50
Royal Caribbean, xiv, 105, 107,
    109–110, 113–116
Rubin, Steve, 129

Rusckowski, Steve, 5, 8

Schecter, Adam, 8
Schwabacher, Richard, 50, 118, 128
Shuren, Jeff, 119
Sills, Alan, 68–69, 88
Sims, Leroy, 55
Sliding Doors, 130
Steinfeld, David, 55, 70
Subotic, Simonida, 13
Supply chain, 7, 21, 26, 41–45, 96,
    129, 139
Swabs, 42–45

Teachers union, 92–93
Thamkittikasem, Jeff, 101
Thermo Fisher Scientific, 34, 120

Titus, Hillary, 21, 50, 85–86
Turn around time, 22, 47-52, 70–72,
    76, 130
Twin testing, 98–99

Wall street journal, 52
Weisberger, Jim, 2–5, 32, 34, 42, 43,
    51, 78–82, 99, 133
Weiss, David, 55
Wizard of Oz, 49
Wolfe, Emma, 101
Wood, Jane, 50, 107–108, 127

Young Frankenstein, 29

Zoltar, 80
Zortman, Dan, 35